FORECASTING FOR MARKET & STRATEGIC DECISIONS

HOW TO:

- Forecast Decisions
- Model Operations
- Project Market Research
- Support Strategic Decision-Making
- Manage Business Cases

Andrew C. Merritt
2016

7-4-16 1043am

ISBN-13: 978-1534744134
ISBN-10: 1534744134

First Edition

FORECASTING FOR MARKET AND STRATEGIC DECISIONS

CONTENTS

PART THREE

MODELING AND FORECASTING

PART FOUR

BUSINESS CASES AND PLANNING

PREFACE

The cover of this book depicts a forest with a path through it. The old *"see the forest for [and not just] the trees"* idiom and the metaphor of *"finding a path through the forest"* are applicable to many aspects of the decision process. And the most important aspect of finding the right path is making a projection about *where the path will lead*, and determining *where you want to go*.

Any decision without a forecast of its implications can be disastrous. Either a personal, business or organizational decision always needs to be evaluated in the context of the particular situation. Unfortunately this is often not the case. For businesses, this is a marketplace model or some sort of operational model. This model need not be overly complicated, but must include all factors that will determine the ultimate outcome, and also account for assumptions (implicitly or explicitly) that are being made about the particular situation or project. Every organization, however large or small, should develop and update models of their administrative, operational, and financial activities, so that they can readily use such models when making forecasts for decisions.

Before any organization makes a decision along with a forecast of what will happen following this decision, it first must clearly state its purpose in a *mission statement.* And along with this mission statement, it needs to define its *business model,* namely the structure of the organization and its relationship to the operating environment.

One should be aware that complex mathematical analysis of historical data does not alone produce a valid forecast. There always needs to be an organized way to account for *assumptions* and *changing conditions* when doing a forecast, and this organized process is itself a model. Based on a sufficient model, projections can guide us in forecasting the future, but historical data alone does not produce a valid forecast.

Of course, judgment and intuition are important elements in predicting the future, but cannot alone be used to forecast. Relying on pure judgment and disregarding *real data* and analysis is a dangerous path to failure and disappointment.

One way to get *real data* is to conduct either primary or secondary market research. This research is often forward-looking, but can also be focused on past events, in order to better understand what has already happened. The main theme of this book is how to properly use market research to predict the future, namely to construct a forecast.

*****

Forecasting itself can be divided into two principal categories: (1) Statistical forecasting that uses historical information in an attempt to predict future trends or events, and (2) Market-based forecasting that uses market research plus market and operational models in order to predict the future.

There are many works on statistical forecasting, so statistical methodology is reviewed only briefly here. The principal caveat is that statistical analysis of past behavior usually is a poor predictor of future behavior and events, since in the most important situations, the environment is dynamic and in fact any important actions or changes will automatically disturb the environment and therefore invalidate past historical data. Sophisticated data crunching will never produce valid results when things will change. This is especially true in today's rich computing environment, where tools and platforms and programs abound, and heads-down analysts can easily get carried away with such data crunching and bean counting, and analysts can delude themselves that historical data alone will reveal the future.

On the other hand, reliance purely on survey information can also take on a life of its own. Sometimes even a raw survey is presented as if it alone is a forecast of the future, and this of course is equally as invalid as the mindless crunching of irrelevant legacy data.

The real answer is a rather pains-taking understanding of the actual environment and then modeling this environment. To do this correctly, we need to capture as much as possible about things like buying behavior, competition, market share, pricing, consumer

8

attitude and cultural changes, distribution and fulfillment, demographics, segments, social changes, customer awareness, promotion and advertising, among many other factors. But we need to keep this all in perspective according to the needs of the problem at hand. There is no point in exhaustive modeling when the change being considered is relatively minor. But when a whole new venture or innovation or major investment is being considered, it is appropriate to develop a broadly comprehensive model of the situation. Often this broad modeling can then be utilized to consider various alternative paths in a business case, and to test assumptions and sensitivity to multiple variables and assumptions. For example, if we spend more on promotion and advertising, how will this affect the forecast? Is there a point of diminishing returns for such expenditures? If we lower or increase price, how will this affect the forecast?

Examples of situations for which we often need to forecast include:

- Introduction of a new product or service

- A change or improvement or new aspects of a product or service

- The outcome of an election or a political process

- A change in a business or governmental policy or regulation

- **A change in a business organizational structure, such as an acquisition or a merger**

- **The future trading price of an investment product, either short-term or long-term**

- **The future trading price of material commodities, such as fossil-based commodities or metal ores or agricultural products**

- **The prices of real estate properties, for either consumer or business real estate, and at the new or resale market level**

- **Crime occurrences, like homicides, robberies, felonies, or drug-related offenses**

Today, a lot of market research is conducted via online panels of respondents who have signed up ahead of time to be paid for their opinions on something. The advantage is efficiency, automatic pre-selection and pre-weighting and qualification of the sample. Also we can reduce the psychological effects of a live face-to-face or telephone interview type of survey. If we have a large database of prospective panelists, who are segmented according to many factors, then online surveys can reduce the confounding effects of the persona and scripting of interviewers. When we have constructed a large database of prospective panelists, the panel for a particular online survey can be appropriately segmented and can be categorized by industry. Then we can quickly survey an appropriate targeted subset of these panelists, and obtain a statistically valid sample.

The disadvantage of online panels can be a bias because such respondents are persons who are comfortable with online and computer-based information-gathering. For example, some buyers could possess a high purchase intent for a product at a particular price, but are either not computer-literate or are highly protective of their identity and resistant to the invasive aspects of an online survey. This bias can apply to many opinion situations.

*****

This book is primarily about microeconomic demand forecasting, as it pertains to markets and decisions. It does not attempt to broach the subject of macroeconomic forecasting, such as for global or country-level economics. It touches on both qualitative and quantitative methodologies, and also statistical and model-based causal forecasting. But there is a bias toward market-model forecasting that is based on market research, either secondary research or primary market research.

The book is divided into *Four Parts*. *Part One* begins with the linking of forecasts to *decisions*, emphasizing that every decision is associated with a direct or implied *forecast*, whether we know it or not. Both *strategic decisions* and administrative/operational decisions are discussed.

Part Two then covers the subject of *market*

research and analysis, which is the the general source of information upon which to base a forecast. The definition of research here is broad, including mining of data from the vast resources available today online, and also secondary market research reports, trade association data, and in many cases both qualitative and quantitative primary research. The emphasis is on managing and integrating all of these information sources, and software to support the process is discussed.

Part Three follows with the subject of *modeling and forecasting*. Modeling of an operational process is covered, such as the marketing of a product or service, and the spirit of the treatment is that the model can vary from something relatively simple to a very complex and comprehensive mathematical formulation. But the over-arching concept is that the model must capture the factors important to the forecast being developed, and the independent variables, like promotion and advertising, must be explicitly included in the model.

Part Four then puts the decision process, research, modeling, and forecasting together as a core element of a *business case* for a proposed initiative, or a complete *business plan* for a new venture or business model proposal.

Related subject material has been placed in the Appendices. *Appendix A* includes a discussion of legacy historical statistical *analysis and trending*, which is often misconstrued as a forecasting tool, but in some cases can be used to develop a starting point for a *forecast base* for model development. *Appendix B* lists a few of the voluminous data mining and secondary research sources available. *Appendix C* summarizes some of the many software platforms available for research, forecasting, and business case support. *Appendix D* lists some of the many very capable market research suppliers that exist, for planning and executing research that will support the market analysis, forecasting, and business planning processes. And lastly, for purely amusement, *Appendix E* includes a few of the many historical forecasts and predictions that turned out to be totally incorrect.

Many readers will want to follow through this book as the various sections are aligned, but it is certainly appropriate to skip around to various topics. Hopefully the book will be of interest to a wide range of readers, and will be useful in the actual practice of developing and utilizing forecasts, be it in business, government, or even personal situations. Best to all in such endeavors!

*****

PART ONE

FORECASTING AND DECISIONS

"If we could first know where we are, then wither we are tending, we could then decide what to do and how to do it" - Abraham Lincoln, June 16, 1858, House Divided Speech, Springfield Illinois State House, Republican Party Convention.

1.1 - DECISIONS IN AN ORGANIZATION

Every decision has consequences. We make a decision and expect a certain outcome. Sometimes this expectation is explicit and very clear. And sometimes this outcome is merely implied but nevertheless expected.

Individuals, organizations, and institutions constantly make decisions and have expectations for the outcome, whether or not they clearly state those expectations. They might or might not be aware that they are forecasting the future. Individuals will have a personal way of making decisions, hopefully in an organized manner, and likewise hopefully an organization will have a complete process for making decisions and forecasts. In either case, decisions and forecasts are intimately linked.

What comes first, the decision or the forecast? Hopefully any decision is made only after the

14

consequences and outcome have been forecasted, but we know that this is unfortunately not always true.

Decisions and forecasts are often based on past experience. We did something before, and a certain outcome occurred, so we often expect that this will happen again. This is true for both individuals and organizations. But we know that this relationship is not always valid. In fact, we often realize that a past decision is no longer going to work, but we go ahead anyway because we are not sure what will happen. Even the most experienced organizations in business, government, politics, and religion do this "try it and see" based on the past. This is because we often do not know how to realistically cope with change and forecast appropriately.

The most successful individuals and organizations *do* realize that things change, so they must have a process for making decisions that are based on accurate forecasts of what will happen. And although they might use past data and experience as a guideline, they will obtain as much new data as possible to forecast the outcome of a decision.

This is true for personal matters, and certainly for legal, financial, and technical matters. But sometimes decisions are made without addressing the future implications of the actions which follow, and sometimes forecasts are stated without focusing on the assumptions that have been made, either directly or indirectly without realization. This can be disastrous for major decisions, or it can be inconsequential for trivial decisions that have little future implications. Sometimes we do not know the difference between what will turn out to be major or what will be trivial.

Some groups or individuals like to make decisions based solely on their judgment, experience, insight or perspectives, without any real data or analysis or understanding of the future. This kind of decision-making has a batting average, and often the individual or group will discount the times that they are wrong about something.

Who Is In Charge?

Decision-making in an organization often has a lot to do with the structure and culture of the entity. In an overly technically-based entity, sometimes decisions are based simply on a belief that a new innovation or invention is so unique that it should be implemented without further evaluation regarding marketability or profitability. And in an overly sales-based entity, a particular customer's request might be implemented without evaluation of the market or financial implications. Also, in an overly financially-based group, sometimes decisions are made purely via "bean-counting" without regard to the market and operational considerations. And in an entity wherein "strategic planning" has an overly-stated control of the organization, sometimes they can identify a new opportunity and declare that it is so strategic that no further evaluation needs to be performed before an implementation decision is reached. Any of these types of purely judgmental and single-minded

16

decisions can have disastrous implications.

Other decision-making individuals or groups can be very risk-averse and can get caught up in analysis-paralysis and never explicitly make a decision because they are afraid of the consequences. Such groups or individuals often wait for events to take control and then react, sometimes too late and to no avail, and then they blame circumstances they declare are beyond their control.

Whatever the decision-making process, every forecast should be optimized to fit the particular need. Too much effort and analysis for a simple decision is inappropriate, but major decisions with far-reaching implications must be based on durable and accurate and well-developed forecasts.

Unfortunately, because of the availability of sophisticated software and virtually unlimited computational capabilities, many decisions today are based primarily on crunching of vast amounts of historical data, without regard to the changes that have taken place since that legacy data was previously developed. This regression trending and data mining can be useful for understanding the past, but it can be a poor predictor of the future. The past gives us a base upon which to further consider our decisions, but the past does not tell us what will happen under changing conditions, namely both things under our control and things largely out of our control, such as actions of competitors or events in the economic and regulatory environment. Today's computing power can better be utilized to understand and model future alternatives.

One of the ways we often try to predict the future is to ask customers, leaders, citizens, buyers, and members of society or a particular group. This interviewing process is complex, since those being interviewed will all have different individual visions of the future, and we must try to bring them all into the same perspective. Equally important is putting their responses in context of the implementation and decision-making process that follows. This requires modeling of the environment, such as the marketplace and operations, as well as societal and cultural considerations. The most important thing to remember about a survey or a poll or market research is that the result of such interviewing is NOT by itself a forecast. A survey can reveal information regarding *market potential*, however we might define this potential, and can be a useful concept in assessing viability and moving toward an actual forecast after a full model of the environment and operations has been developed.

Therefore, whether we directly recognize or disregard the relationship between forecasts and decisions, the two are intimately related. Decisions can change the future and good decisions should be based on a view of the future implications, namely a forecast. One affects the other.

Lastly, the decision process is often based on a *business case*, and this business case must be the complete integration of research, forecasting, modeling, and assumption-building, so that it all fully supports the proposed decision. Without such integration, the decision process will be flawed and success will not be achieved.

1.2 - STRATEGIC DECISIONS

It is useful to think of some decisions as *"strategic"* in that such decisions will have far-reaching implications. In the business environment, we refer to the structure of an enterprise or business deal as the *"business model,"* but this term applies equally to all organizations, such as governmental or academic entities. Regarding business models, any decision which changes the business model of an enterprise is automatically a strategic decision. For example, a business that has been operating as a sole proprietorship that decides to form a partnership with others is making a strategic decision. The decision will affect all future executive actions as well as market and operational activities. Another example is changing the name of an entity or the brand of an offering. This might at first seem like a simple decision, but it can have far-reaching implications that affect customer awareness, market share, sales, revenues and profitability. Remember when Coca-Cola introduced in April 1985 the "New Coke" brand for which they changed the chemical formula for the drink, and the market rejected the change. They had to return to basically the original sweeter formula in July 1985. Some managers at Coke might have thought that this decision was a relatively minor addition to the mix of offerings, but either they did not forecast the full implications, or their forecasting and market research

19

were grossly in error.

Sometimes corporations rush into a decision that is certainly strategic, but they fail to understand the implications. For example, AT&T made two major decisions which did not work out, because they did not properly forecast the tactical and strategic issues that were involved. They acquired the NCR Corporation in 1991 for $7.4B and in 1996 spun off NCR as again a separate entity, after a period of substantial losses and headcount reductions. NCR's original customers included competitors of AT&T and after the AT&T acquisition, these customers became reluctant to buy from a competitor's subsidiary. A second AT&T strategic decision that did not work was the acquisition of TCI (Tele-Communications Inc., a cable TV group) in 1999 for $48B but AT&T sold it off to Comcast in 2002 for $44B and got out of the cable TV business. It turned out that TCI had put together a number of local cable systems around the U.S., many of which would require major upgrades to move to a full broadband communications capability. This fact was either not identified or a forecast of the costs and implications was not developed.

Appendix E includes numerous historical examples of decisions and predictions, many of which were certainly strategic, all of which were incorrect forecasts and predictions.

To better assist in an understanding of strategic decisions, here are some examples of decisions, primarily business-related, which have strategic implications:

20

- Changing the overall business model from in-house manufacturing to leasing-out of intellectual properties and outsourcing of production

- Bypassing distributors and wholesalers by becoming a direct or online retailer

- Merger-acquisitions of most any nature

- Diversification to an entirely new market segment

- Spinoff of an area of business via an IPO stock offering or sale to another entity

- Forming a joint venture

- Deciding to not develop and market a major in-house R&D innovation, and either licensing it off or merely dropping the program without follow-up

- Changing all pricing plans and-or revising all prices up or down

- Ending all retail operations and becoming a wholesaler

- Outsourcing and/or offshoring

In contrast, here are some business decisions which are purely *administrative* and *operational*:

- **Adding some manufacturing capacity to meet demand**

- **Increasing or decreasing advertising budgets**

- **Changing advertising themes but to the same targeted market segments**

- **Altering the advertising media mix, e.g. online versus TV versus print**

- **Redesigning product labels but keeping brand identification**

- **Changing wholesalers and distributors for a better deal**

- **Reorienting the channel mix to match priorities**

Note that all of these administrative and operational changes and decisions *will change forecasts* and could have anywhere from a minor to a major impact on things. But these are tactical and execution decisions, not to be categorized as strategic.

What Is Strategic?

A strategic decision often changes both the *mission statement* and the *business model* of an entity. This could mean going from a proprietership to a joint venture or a public corporation. Or it could mean an acquisition into a new market segment or an acquisition that adds new brands and innovations to the entity's mix of offerings, thereby addressing new segments. Anything beyond purely administrative and operational decisions usually has strategic implications and needs to be properly treated as such. Some have defined "strategic" as a large action which has long term implications, and although this is generally true, it is only one element defining of the overall strategic category of decisions.

One way to evaluate a strategic decision is to create scenarios for *before* and *after* the strategic decision is actually implemented, and to analyze the difference. Also, alternative opportunities and scenarios are often generated. If a decision is strategic in nature, there often will be legal and regulatory matters to be evaluated, in addition to the market and financial aspects.

Maintain an Ongoing Portfolio of Strategic Alternatives

It is useful to maintain an ongoing portfolio of strategic alternatives and associated models for an entity. That way, there will not be any frantic and schedule-challenged efforts to support a strategic decision that is under consideration. Of course, this is not always possible, if an opportunity should arise suddenly and unexpectedly. But at least there might be some alternatives and models which have been previously developed and analyzed which could provide a starting point for any proposed strategic decision which must be properly analyzed immediately.

23

Acquisitions, Mergers, Divestitures, and Due Diligence

When an acquisition, a merger, or a divestiture is being considered, usually there is a phase called "*due diligence*," which purports to find out as much as possible about the entities, both before and after, including *valuations*. The valuation process looks at: (1) Tangible hard assets, like real estate, buildings, factories, facilities, inventories, and raw materials on hand; and (2) Intangibles, like customer accounts, patents, licensing agreements, personnel, brand equity, supply chain agreements, and intellectual property. Customer accounts are where the money is, that is, the source of revenue, and these need to be forecasted for both the current environment and for the environment after a potential acquisition. Income statements and balance sheets need to be constructed and projected for both before and after the proposed acquisition. So both direct costs like facilities and labor, and also indirect costs like allocated overheads, general advertising, and human resources need to be forecasted in this projected going-forward view. All of this needs to follow a consistent set of assumptions across revenue, costs and assets. Valuation is best done utilizing models and analytical methods and sensitivity analysis, but some aspects of valuation can be based on intuitive and knowledge-based assessments.

As in real estate, valuation is sometimes done indirectly by looking at "*comparables*," namely, other situations like companies in the same industry or other recent acquisitions and mergers.

24

So for all types of strategic decisions, forecasts are extremely important. But unfortunately, there are many examples where strategic decisions have been made without adequately forecasting the estimated results of the decision.

Elements Of A Strategic Decision

It is useful, if not mandatory, to break a strategic decision into a number of steps. Grossly, any strategic decision can be broken down into two Main Steps:

(1) FIRST STEP: Mission Statement and Business Model Decisions

(2) SECOND STEP: Implementation Decisions

Of course, alternatives must be considered regarding both of the above Main Steps. And usually security and confidentiality and ethics overlay both of these Steps.

The *Mission Statement* of an entity is not fixed and immutable over time, but must be kept up to date, especially in the face of environmental, technological, regulatory, competitive and operational changes. For example, automobile manufacturers who confine themselves to internal combustion cars and reject hybrid and electric car alternatives can find themselves losing out on new opportunities. And entities that were late in considering e-commerce and distribution via the Internet in many cases lost market share to others.

The First Step cannot be considered lightly. For a sole-proprietorship, there may be only one or a few persons involved in the decision. But in many entities, there is a range of stakeholders who are affected by any decision to modify the mission statement and business model. Investors, partners, and employees themselves will be affected and must be considered. It has been said that once a business or an individual decides to do something, then they should not ask lawyers and accountants what to do, but rather how to do it.

Once a strategic decision is brought into concert with decisions regarding the mission statement and business model of an entity, many strategic decisions will follow regarding Implementation of the First Step. In this Second Step, many questions must be addressed, like:

(1) Is this the right time to go ahead with implementation of an agreed-upon change in the mission statement and business model?

(2) Does the current company have cash on hand to do a major acquisition, or is it to be done via a stock transfer? If via stock transfer, what will the dilution effect be and the consequences?

(3) Or, just because the mission statement and business model will be changed, is the best alternative to *do nothing* at this time and monitor all aspects and then choose the optimal conditions for implementation.

(4) Are there overpowering regulatory or legislative considerations that could hinder or obstruct an implementation? Or conversely, have regulatory changes opened up new opportunities?

(5) If an acquisition or merger fits the mission statement and business model, can a target entity be found at this time? How will we find such an entity? Will this be a hostile takeover or does the mission statement confine any such action to a win-win situation only?

(6) If a divestiture fits the mission statement, is this to be done by creating a new entity, either public (IPO) or private, or merely selling to an interested party, if such exists?

(7) How open and transparent should the implementation process be? Namely. would it be better to inform all stakeholders throughout the process, or should all decisions be closely held until everything has been resolved and confirmed and then an announcement is ready to go?

1.3 - FINDING NEW OPPORTUNITIES

Closely related to decision-making and forecasting in an organization is the responsibility for identifying new business opportunities. The healthy organization never sits back complacently. thinking that a current highly profitable situation will last forever. Technical innovations, regulatory changes, competitive actions, and customer attitudes can change rapidly. The flexible and nimble organization must recognize changes in time to adapt, survive and thrive. In the best well-functioning organizations, everybody is always on the lookout for new opportunities and changes, although sometimes one particular department, like market management or strategic planning will play a dominant role.

It is useful that, when in support of all other organizational entities, those responsible for forecasting adopt a *proactive forecasting* role. That is, rather than wait until market research and forecasting requests are expressed by particular clients and research sponsors, that a forecasting organization should identify and publicize any new marketplace opportunities and trends which they have recognized in their monitoring of the environment, attending industry conferences, and overall data mining activities.

This proactive forecasting can be done in several ways. Internal communications via email or occasional seminars can be utilized, and sometimes outside speakers and experts can be invited to express their views and speak of new opportunities.

However it is structured and implemented, every organization needs to have a well-organized process for identifying new opportunities. That is, this activity should not be dominated by hearsay and haphazard contacts, but rather should follow a process which identifies, captures, publicizes, and evaluates new opportunities and keeps up-to-date records and documentation. The goal is to not miss out on anything that has great potential for the organization, and to never be caught off guard by a competitive or industry trend or announcement.

1.4 - FORECASTING FOR DECISIONS

Forecasting is a critical element of the human reasoning process. Child development begins with an innate capability to learn the future implications of decisions, starting with small childhood actions. And throughout the human lifecycle, there is at least a capability to return to previously learned reasoning, and at best a lifelong ability to better understand the future implications of our decisions.

Market forecasting has been occurring as long as human commerce - it was merely judgmental in early days. How much should be produced? How much will sell? Merchants often merely produced a quantity that they could carry on camels and horses and in caravans and then went out to sell this until depletion, and adjusted price along the way - they went by hearsay and speculation on prices, but when middlemen became involved and brokers came into play then they had to know how much to produce, to order, to stock, to inventory, and how much would sell within a given period of time.

All forecasting begins with a *conceptualization* of

the problem or situation. This is true for individuals and also for groups and organizations. In the idealized business decision process, conceptualization is followed by contextualizing the decision, including all aspects of the environment, such as the marketplace, regulation, technology, and economic conditions. Third, information is gathered from existing or new sources, including data mining, competitive analysis, review of secondary research, and formulation and conducting of new primary market research when appropriate. This is followed by assumption-building, then modeling and formulation of the decision and its implementation, plus mechanization and calculation of forecasts. Next, calculated outputs are analyzed and iterations are made as required. For major decisions, a full business plan and proposal is prepared and circulated and approved. Lastly, a program or project is launched, actions occur, and tracking of actual results is compared to the forecasts and assumptions that had been made.

On the next page is a simple diagram of these basic steps of a Forecasting Process.

FIGURE 1

THE MOST BASIC FORECAST MODEL

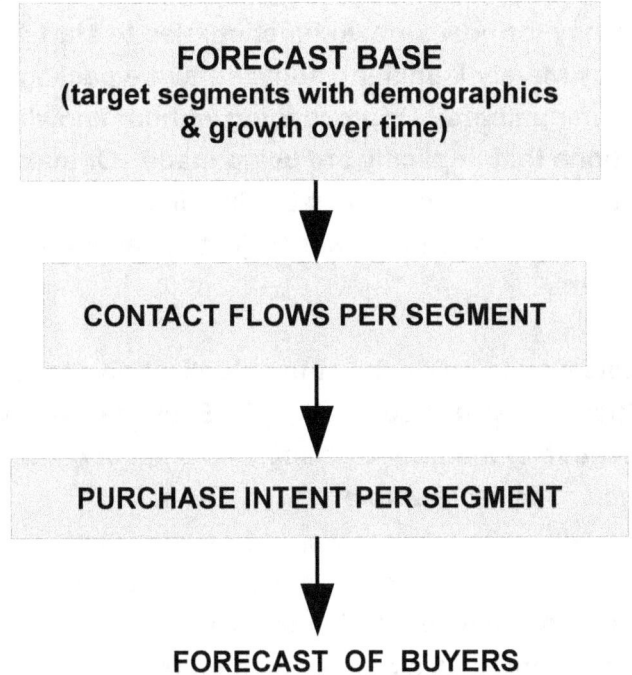

FORECAST BASE
(target segments with demographics
& growth over time)

CONTACT FLOWS PER SEGMENT

PURCHASE INTENT PER SEGMENT

FORECAST OF BUYERS

Proper conceptualization is perhaps the most important element of the forecasting process.
If we do not correctly formulate what we need at the start of the process, a forecast can go in the wrong direction, or we could even end up forecasting the wrong things. If the forecast is to be used in a business case or business plan, it must be determined what will be appropriate for the overall needs, including the goals, objectives, scheduling

and budgeting of the project or program and organization.

Conceptualization is by definition thoroughly thinking through the environment and the context of the forecast. With today's processing power, we must avoid the tendency for heads-down functionaries to start a forecast by merely launching some software package and plugging in numbers. Or proceeding without knowing the assumptions that implicitly are being made. Or making assumptions without obtaining the buy-in of others affected, such as members of a project team and financial stakeholders.

One way to guide the conceptualization process is to conduct an *"event-tree analysis." (Event-tree analysis is a derivative of the fault-tree analysis used in quality assurance. See for example https://en.wikipedia.org/wiki/Fault_tree_analysis)* A decision can be parsed into events and actions which will follow from the decision, both positive and negative. Then secondary events and actions which follow from the first level are identified. This is followed by tertiary events and actions, and so forth, on down to the most basic level. Here is a simple diagram of an event-tree process that can guide conceptualization.

Figure 2

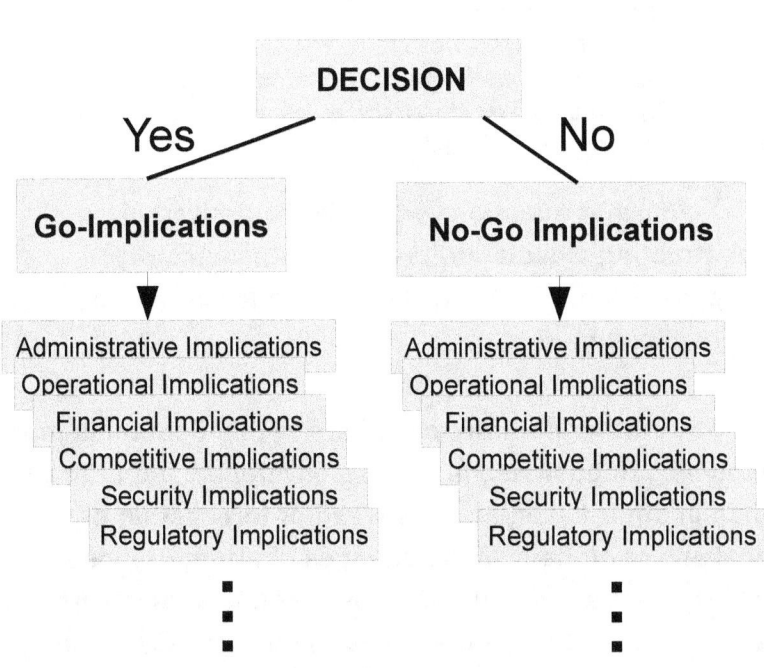

As an example, suppose we wanted to use a decision-tree to analyze the decision to build a new factory. We would create a diagram which addressed the following types of questions.

> *"DECISION TO BUILD A NEW FACTORY"*
> *Questions to be addressed:*
> 1. *How soon is the new capacity required?*
> 2. *What assumptions were used to determine the new capacity requirements?*
> 3. *Is there a buy-in by all stakeholders for this decision?*
> 4. *Have all regulatory and legal matters been resolved?*
> 5. *Is the build-decision better than outsourcing to increase capacity?*

6. *What are the outsourcing options?*
7. *Can outsourcing be a stopgap action to meet capacity schedules?*
8. *Can we expand one or more existing factories?*
9. *Can second or third shifts be added or are they already exhausted?*

Further questions would be addressed in constructing a decision-tree for the "new factory proposal," until the team responsible for this program was fully satisfied.

Another point to make here in this Section is that *modeling* in business is far less developed and utilized than in other fields, such as weather forecasting or analysis of global climate changes. In both of these cases, giant supercomputers are used to analyze massive amounts of both satellite and land-sensor data. Some other supercomputer demos of note include the IBM Deep Blue chess computer victory over the Master Gary Kasparov, and the IBM Watson computer Jeopardy prize victory. Some day quantum computing and other advances will make business supercomputers commonplace and inexpensive, and then full modeling and forecasting will be the norm. Meanwhile, we need to do the best to incorporate modeling and forecasting into corporate and other organizational decision-making. We know that macroeconomic modeling has often failed to predict national or global economic cycles, and microeconomic modeling is seldom properly applied in business. Hopefully business microeconomic modeling and forecasting for decision-making will increase in the future.

In the Sections which follow, all the steps of the above forecasting process will be discussed in detail, but the following additional Section is added here to emphasize the importance of forecasts in business decisions.

1.5 MARKET POTENTIAL FOR DECISION-MAKING

Sometimes we can base a decision merely on the *market potential* for an idea, such as an innovation or a product or service. For example, in a *phased-development process,* the decision to proceed to the next phase of development might merely require that an update to the market potential be stated, rather than a forecast of the eventual demand itself. If the perspective of the organization, be it in government, business, or academia, is that *investment spending* be devoted to the exploration and development of a new area, then *market potential,* rather than eventual actual demand can be deemed sufficient to proceed in the here-and-now. In other words, to take a chance and proceed, until we know more and will make further decisions.

Market potential can be derived from secondary sources such as authoritative secondary market research reports, from the analysis of data mining information, or from qualitative research like properly conducted focus group sessions.

And often it is a good idea to compose a "back-of-th-envelope" business case to go along with any market potential effort. This way we can keep track of what the

35

initiative is worth, until we know more details.

1.6 - APPLICATIONS OF FORECASTS IN DECISIONS

Forecasts support decisions in strategic, administrative and operational matters. This is true in business, governmental, religious, and academic domains, and regarding the full range of financial, legal, regulatory, human resources, marketing, and manufacturing matters.

To emphasize this, here are some further examples of forecast applications, divided into *strategic*, *administrative*, and *operational* categories.

Strategic Forecast Examples

- Revenues, expenses, and margins both before and after merger and acquisition proposals

- Revenues, expenses, and margins both before and after a proposed regulatory change

- Forecasts in support of a joint venture proposal

- Forecasts in support of a decision to vacate an entire market segment

- Forecasts in response to a major legal challenge, like an anti-trust action

- Forecasts in support of a decision to increase stock

dividends or to reinvest among R&D, administrative, and operations proposals

Administrative Forecast Examples

- The forecasted effects of a staff reduction

- The forecasted awareness and revenue gain for an advertising or promotion campaign

- The forecasted revenue and margin gain for increasing the number of retail distributors

- The forecasted effects of a training program

- The forecasted effects of a new recruitment program

- Human resources forecasts for budgeting and benefits requirements

- The forecasted effect of an increased help desk capability

- The forecasted effects of a warranty change

- Forecasts in support of prioritizing features and functions for a new product or service

- Sales forecasts, in support of the budgeting process and sales management

- **Budgetary forecasts, in support of the annual planning cycle, and borrowing requirements**

- **Forecasts in support of RFP and bid responses**

- **Unsolicited customer business plan forecasts in support of sales expansion and prospecting**

Operational Forecast Examples

- **The forecasted effects of a factory closing or offshore relocation**

- **The forecasted effects to decide on an outsourcing program proposal**

- **Forecasts in support of a decision to lease-out or manufacture in-house, a new innovation**

- **Forecasts to support a decision among subcontractor bids**

- **Forecasts for manufacturing, production, and subcontracting vendor requirements**

- **Forecasts to support corporate floor-space and building requirements decisions**

*****

PART TWO

MARKET RESEARCH AND ANALYSIS

2.1 CLIENTS, SPONSORS, AND STAKEHOLDERS

The research for an idea, an innovation, an initiative, or merely to get a clear understanding of something, can take many forms. Sometimes we want to know about attitudes regarding past events, or how persons previously arrived at a certain choice or made a previous purchase. But often research is conducted in support of an *upcoming* decision. We can ask those who will be directly affected by a decision, either informally and individually or in groups, or we can ask statistically valid samples of a targeted or universal demographic group, what they think. However such research is conducted, it must be very purposeful, organized, and follow a *well-defined process*. Otherwise, the result of the research will not be meaningful, time will be wasted, and very likely incorrect decisions will result.

The reader of this book could be in a research department within an enterprise or a governmental agency, or some other entity like a consulting firm, or even a religious institution, and of course perhaps a staff member of a market research supplier. Therefore, the clients, sponsors, and stakeholders of any primary market research will vary widely. If you are in a central market

39

research organization within a large business entity, then you might have many in-house clients in other departments, like product management, market management, advertising and promotion, human resources, manufacturing, finance, strategic planning, and even the board of directors. Sometimes each operating unit of a large and diversified enterprise will have their own in-house research units, or merely a separate skeleton staff that outsources to a research supplier on their own budget. Sometimes competitive analysis needs to be conducted via a primary research project, and this needs to be closely held in the organization, and will be budgeted and kept confidential accordingly. And suppose a strategic study needs to be conducted to determine alternatives for diversification or merger-acquisition possibilities, and this type of market research will also be very confidential and budgeted and managed accordingly.

It is almost the rule that whoever has the *budget* for market research will be in charge and will determine the needs and parameters of the research, but there can be exceptions also. Just because an entity controls the budget does not always mean that they have the knowledge and perspective to set up and manage the research properly. The worst and most wasteful management of research is when an entity feels the pressure of a schedule, and charges off with a half-baked research effort that not only misses many important questions, but also can result in totally incorrect findings and disastrously wrong decisions. When other stakeholders who were not consulted see the results, they will refuse buy-in for the project, and either nothing will happen or implementation will be greatly flawed. You do not want to be involved in such misguided activities, because eventually there will a diagnosis and assignment of blame for those who were involved.

2.2 THE INTEGRATED PROCESS

Market research is not just an isolated activity within an organization, but rather it is one element of a total process, either for developing a forecast or a set of forecasts, or as an important part of a business case or business plan. The diagram on the next page, Figure 3, illustrates the major inter-relationships among research, forecasting, and a business case.

FIGURE 3

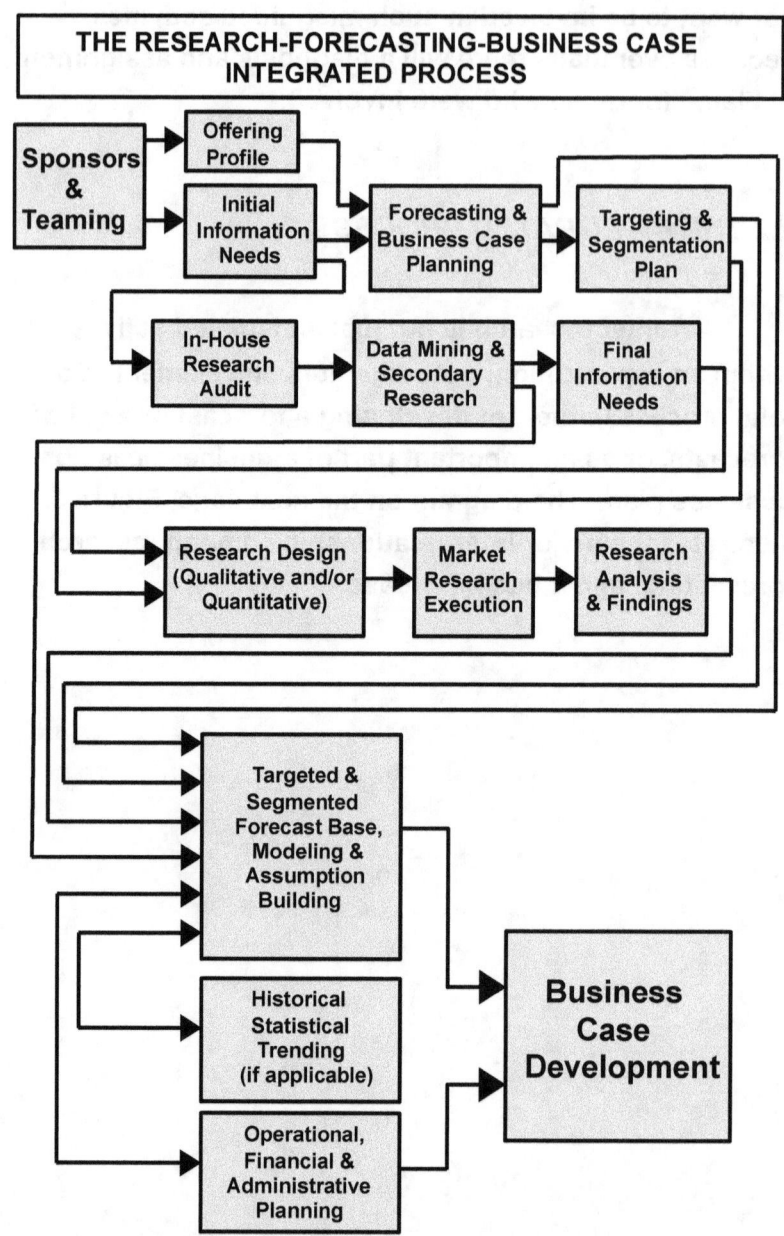

THE RESEARCH-FORECASTING-BUSINESS CASE INTEGRATED PROCESS

The most important point regarding the above flow diagram of the *integrated process* is that market research must be planned according to *"what we are going to do with the research results ?"* In many cases, the output of research will be incorporated into a business case or a full business plan. But sometimes research is intended merely to fulfill certain informational needs for further planning, or merely for a forecast to correct, assist, or support implementation. We need to avoid the classic mistake of doing market research only to find out that the results do not fit the next steps in an integrated modeling, forecasting, and business case process.

In the above flow diagram, the start or any research process is always via the *sponsors* of the research, plus the initial team associated with such sponsoring. Sometimes the sponsors are highly knowledgeable regarding market research projects, and sometimes they are totally naive and might state unreasonable and inconsistent needs. And of course, they may or may not have the budget or the final authority to approve the research project. All of this needs to be worked out in the beginning of any research project, so that the whole project initiates properly and does not later become un-hooked, derailed, interrupted, or even terminated prematurely.

Teaming For Determining Information Needs

Before proceeding with any new market research project, it is mandatory to establish the *goals and objectives* for this research, and to make sure that there is buy-in from all affected stakeholders. This is best done by assembling a team that spans the organization, and bringing them up to speed on the overall business case or offering program, and then soliciting ideas and information requirement according to their individual perspectives. The members of this team should be very knowledgeable regarding the needs of their individual departments, but should be aware that at any first meeting that nothing is being finalized and that eventually the research project will decide on the exact questions to be addressed.

So the first thing that the sponsors need to state is their *Initial Information Needs* and also the *Offer Profile*. The initial information needs start with the raw requests of the sponsors, but are boiled-down at least initially until further phases in the research planning process when the final information needs are established. The Offer Profile does not need to be a new product or service offering, but could be some important change in pricing, billing, fulfillment, branding, merchandising, positioning, targeting or advertising and promotion. Sometimes the offer profile change to be researched will involve the business model, like transitioning to a franchise model and therefore expanding locations, or even a joint venture of some sort.

Information Needs and the *Offer Profile* are then both important elements in the *Forecasting and Research Planning* phase, as indicated in the flow diagram. The important research planning phase usually includes a full teaming with the research supplier (if outsourced), the research sponsors, product managers, market managers, operational managers, financial managers, and representatives of all the stakeholders that will be involved with the offering. One important output of the Forecasting and Research Planning phase will be the *Targeting And Segmentation Plan.* Clearly not every segment, or household, or individual, or fulfillment entity will be researched, but rather a carefully selected group of target segments. Usually this is done conservatively, knowing that additional segments will also eventually have interest in the offering, but sometimes we might want to explore certain unknown segments, especially for an entirely new type of offering.

The Market Research Audit

Note that in the above Integrated Process, the initial information needs must be evaluated first against a *Research Audit* to determine if such information is already readily available in-house as the result of any other recent research project. This might seem trivial, but in many large organizations, there are competing in-house fiefdoms who fund their own research and have just asked the same questions with the same category of respondents. To be fair, such redundant research might be flawed and have to be redone, or the offering might have been improved by another department.

As an example, a *Market Research Audit* should cover the following kinds of questions:

45

Example Market Research Audit Questions

- **Have you ever done research on this type of problem before? If so, when? Is it still valid or has a lot changed?**

- **Has anybody else or any other department ever done research on this type of problem before? If so, when?**

- **Is this a very first-time market research effort, or has your organization been doing market research for many years?**

- **Does your organization have its own in-house research capabilities, or are your market research projects outsourced?**

- **Even if you have been doing market research in-house for a long time, could working with an experienced outside market research service add value and keep you up to date on new methodologies and data sources?**

- **Are multiple research projects being managed at the same time?**

- **Do you have a cross-organizational market research team in order to identify needs of all stakeholders?**

- **Who pays for market research in your**

organization? Do product managers, strategic planners, and others have their own budgets for market research, or is there a central research organization that can fund everybody's negotiated research needs?

- Do you identify market research goals and needs on a regular basis or merely on a one-off basis?

- Do you have a robust market and operational modeling capability to fully incorporate research results into the organization?

- Do you utilize a mix of market research modes, appropriate to the particular project and goals, and your own organizational structure?

- Do you have a very secure market research information environment? If you outsource to a research supplier, do you have security safeguards? Do you utilize cloud services and online research and panel services which house some of your proprietary research information?

- Do you have a system for monitoring competitors, and also for assuring security in regard to competitor knowledge?

- Do you regularly conduct a Market Research Audit covering the above types or questions? If so, can you compare current Audit results to past Audits of the market research process?

After a Research Audit is conducted, it is important to thoroughly review available *Secondary Research*, plus conduct a *Data Mining* task to evaluate the vast amount of governmental and industry data that is available. After these steps are completed, the *Final Information Needs* will be properly cleansed and established for research planning.

As indicated in the above Integrated Research Process Flow Diagram in Figure 3, the major integration of the steps that have been discussed so far is now the *Modeling And Forecasting* task. Also, two important additional inputs need to be factored into this Modeling. First, any applicable *Historical Statistical Analysis* must be considered, with the proviso that the past will usually not predict the future unless nothing has changed, and then of course, there will be no need for new market research. (*Appendix A* includes a discussion of Legacy Historical Statistical Analysis.) The second important category of inputs to the Forecasting and Modeling task are the *Operational, Financial, and Administrative Plans*. These plans will primarily be key inputs to a business case, but might have bearing on the modeling and forecasting also.

Some market research projects will be intended to produce a forecast or a range of forecasts for an offering, and the flow process indicated will terminate at this point. But often, even if it is a "back of the envelope business case" the research findings, modeling, forecasting, and the implementation plans will then be included in the *Business Case Development* process, as indicated in the final element in the above integrated research flow diagram. (Part Four of this book will cover business case development in detail.)

So to summarize, a market research project does not stand alone, but is an important element of an integrated process. The above flow diagram should be considered merely as an example of this integration, and such integration must be specifically tailored to the organization that is sponsoring and requesting any market research, including how they operate, who makes decisions, what has been done in the past, and what new ideas and elements should be included in any updated research process. However all this is accomplished, it is very important to note that failure to integrate the market research process is dangerous, and can result in researching the wrong things, wasting time and money, and eventually making incorrect decisions and incurring failure.

2.3 MARKET RESEARCH PLANNING & DESIGN

The previous Section emphasized the importance of an integrated market research process, and now we will consider the major steps to be followed in actually planning a market research project.

The In-House Or Supplier Contracting Decision

Even if a market research supplier has been used in the past for most all research needs, it is a good idea to pose the question for every new project, regarding in-house or outsourcing of the research. And since new suppliers are constantly available, the question of sole-sourcing or bidding the project should also be addressed. It is not just price but also capabilities and deliverables that must be assessed.

If you do want to utilize a market research supplier, they should be brought into the process as early as possible, and be part of the team, not just after you feel that you have decided on your information needs. The supplier can add value to your decision process, and they very well might have done a similar research project in the past and can make valuable suggestions.

Market research suppliers need to sign a Confidentiality and Non-Compete Agreement at the highest level of their organization, assuring that your research will be managed with the highest levels of confidentiality and security. For example, you can specify that they will not subcontract work via offshoring to others who are distant from your knowledge and control, and will often pose the greatest threat to security. This should be a separate document from the Supplier Contract, but referenced in the Contract. Usually suppliers have their staffs supporting several clients at the same time. You can ask that their representatives be dedicated exclusively to your project for the duration, if the project is of high dollar value and importance to your organization. You can also request that they do not contract with any other organization which is your direct competitor, and specify a long time frame before they might bid on or contract with such competitors. But always probe the supplier and get as much in writing as possible.

When investigating various market research suppliers, you should always get three or more bids for the project, even if you are familiar with certain research suppliers from past projects. New firms appear all the time and old firms are constantly adding to their capabilities. Also, ask for references and testimonials and talk to prior clients of the supplier.

The advantages of using outside market research suppliers can be great. They keep in touch with the latest developments in research including methodologies, software, and data sources. If they worked with you in the past, you might know members of their staff and this will assist in the overall teaming effort.

Security And Confidentiality Of Market Research

Security and confidentiality of market research is extremely important in today's environment. Not only do your competitors want to know what potential products and services that you are exploring, but there are other worldwide hackers and spies who want to obtain any information that they can and either use directly or broker off to others. Don't be naive about this.

Cloud Services and Online Surveys and Online Panels are highly in vogue today. But these open up new security questions compared to conducting all aspects of market research in-house.

Every organization should have a document security process and in particular for market research that you conduct.

A listing of *some* of the major market research suppliers is contained in *Appendix D*, but you should also review the *Market Research Association* (Reference 1) and *GreenBook (*Reference 2) websites, among other directories of suppliers that are listed in Appendix D.

Selection Of Research Modes

The market research method chosen for a particular need must always fit the problem. This is a critical part of the *Market Research Planning* task that is included in the Integrated Research Planning flow diagram of Figure 3.

First, there are generally *Three Categories* of market research, namely:

1. INFORMATIONAL RESEARCH
2. RESEARCH FOR FORECASTING
3. RESEARCH FOR A BUSINESS CASE

Informational Research often can be qualitative, and based on Focus Group sessions or individual respondent interviews. It provides a general idea of opinions, attitudes, likes and dislikes, product concept acceptance, and so forth. The participants need not be end-user consumers, and sometimes are conducted with technical experts, opinion leaders, senior executives, investors, regulators, persons in the supply chain, or administrative or operational personnel. But it is important to note that qualitative research provides only ideas and directions, and can *never* be used to forecast trends or demand, because this research is typically a small sample, and responses usually are not coded against targeted segments or a disciplined demographic profile. Sometimes focus groups can be used to educate the research sponsor themselves, to advise them of the general environment, and to set up the next step of quantitative market research. Often sponsors will view a well-moderated focus group session behind a one-way glass mirror, so as to not disturb the focus group process, and often such sessions are videotaped for later reference.

Informational Research does not always have to be done via live focus groups, and can be conducted in other ways, such as via a random emailing or a random paper mailing, or via random or directed telephone interviews. Online Panels can also be used for qualitative, informational research, but if the questions are largely open-ended to gather opinions, then forecasting is again not advised, even if the online panel sample is quite large.

The above second category of research, namely *Market Research for Forecasting,* always must be quantitative and highly structured. The selection and targeting of respondents must match the Market Research Plan, as developed per the flow of Figure 3. When results are obtained, they must always be *weighted* to account for any *under-representation* or *over-representation* of all of the cells that are determined by the targeting, segmentation, forecast base, and demographic elements that were established in the Research Plan. It used to be that such quantitative market research was usually done via personal one-on-one interviews, either through Mall-Intercept or Telephone Outbound Calling, or Mailed Questionnaires. But today, Online Panels provide a very useful and rapid way to conduct quantitative research. These Panels already have pre-certified segmentation and demographic data on the respondents, and geographic metro-market selection can be well controlled without having to travel to many locations. Data collection can be fully automated and mechanized, so that tedious coding is avoided. Scripting uniformity is assured, and any persona-bias of the interviewer can be eliminated because the research is self-administered and the Panel respondents are not entering into a face-to-face or live voice response session.

However, Online Panels open up many security questions, since essentially this is a cloud-based service, and the raw data reside on servers beyond the direct control of the research sponsors. Often there is outsourcing of the IT elements of the platforms, and even with non-disclosure agreements and confidentiality agreements, there can be a concern that the research data could fall into the wrong hands, such as competitors or hackers. This is especially true in the case of offshoring for processing or data backup.

Another factor to consider regarding Online Panels is the respondent bias that comes from those harboring computer-fright or those who are guarded against invasive surveying of their demographics, their attitudes, and their preferences. Sometimes, such computer-fright individuals might have previously experienced hacking incidents or identity theft. Such individuals might well at the same time be perfectly valid buyers or decision-makers. Also, remember that some bias might come from the fact that most Panel participants are paid respondents. Sometimes a check question can be included to evaluate these concerns, but this bias factor regarding Online Panels should be recognized.

Third in the *Market Research Category* categories that were listed above, many market research projects are part of a *Business Case Development Process.* All of the elements just discussed regarding *Research For Forecasting* must be followed correctly when research is to be used to support a business case, knowing that eventually in any final decision-making, that the research will be brought into question, and sensitivity questions and alternative scenarios will come into play. For a Strategic Decision this is even more important. Therefore, it is important that the research for supporting a business case or business plan include questions that relate to all of the variables that will be modeled in the analysis, such as things like the business model of the proposed program, branding and joint venture identification, co-marketing, supply chain elements, advertising and promotion, and so forth. If these things are left out of the research, then it will be impossible to answer questions regarding sensitivities and alternatives, which inevitably arise when a key executive decision to approve a business plan must be made.

Some Additional Market Research Methods

There are many variations on the Three Primary Market Research Categories that have just been discussed. Here is a list of some of these variations, but new methods and ideas for research are constantly being creatively devised.

Pre-Scheduled In-Office Executive Interviews: When the survey responses are important and the respondents are middle-level or officer-level executives, it is sometimes possible to get them to schedule an interview session in their office. The interviewer needs to be very professional and conversant in the particular industry terminology and issues. The executives being interviewed will be highly concerned about competitive and security issues, and only qualitative results can be expected.

Trade Conference Private Interviews: Often at any trade show, there will be off-the-floor private interview rooms available so that key executives that happen to be attending the conference can be invited to come to a room for further discussion of initiatives, new offerings, and particular issues. Such executives are looking for possible new opportunities for their company, but will expect a sales-pitch environment. Their responses are qualitative, and they will be defensive about privacy, security, and competitive factors. Sometimes third-party consultants will roam a trade show floor looking to bring key executives to such a private room, so that they possibly can find a new consulting client or obtain a finders-fee.

Email Surveys: Instead of interviewing respondents either live face-to-face or in a live telephone interview, email questionnaires can be sent out to a pre-determined and properly targeted and segmented list of respondents. Of course, if this is merely an unsolicited broadcasted email, then the results will have multiple bias factors, and can only be considered qualitative and totally unweighted, and often unreliable. Such unsolicited emails are generally considered spamming and will either be blocked by email providers, firewall software, or be in violation of regulations, and in any case can have a low response rate.

Telephone Surveys: These can be live outbound calls from a market research interviewing call center to a pre-segmented list, or merely random outbound calls. The sessions can be at a pre-arranged appointment time to which the respondents have agreed, or could be at random times during the day or early evening hours. The sessions usually have to be of limited duration, or the respondents will terminate before the end of the script and the results will be incomplete and not very useful. Also, only limited demographic information is possible, so that weighting corrections will be limited, and forecasting will be unreliable and not recommended.

Robo-Calls: There is much computer-based software today to conduct random automated and mechanized outbound telephone surveys, referred to as "robocalls," that is, robotic call surveys. These usually are set up to call all 10,000 numbers in a local telephone exchange, and respondents are asked to respond to a pre-arranged robotic script, or even a number of rotated scripts. There will be many incompletes and demographics are merely by location and zip code for the respondents' local telephone exchanges. Results are unreliable and qualitative only.

Survey Mailers: Seldom used anymore, surveys can be done via paper in a mailed-out package, and either can be directed to a narrow and well-defined mailing list or merely a random mailing. Incompletes and non-returns will be high, and of course results are only qualitative at best.

Mall-Intercept: This is a term used to denote face-to-face interviews that are conducted in private rooms hidden within shopping malls. Agents for the research supplier will roam the mall looking for respondents who appear to fit particular demographic cells (age, sex, etc.) and will invite them to come to an interview room for a survey session. The usual attempt is to have enough raw unweighted completed sessions, that then can be corrected and used for quantitative analysis and forecasting. Mall-Intercept can also be used to obtain focus group respondents, for qualitative research.

Test Market Research: When the sponsors of the research wish to obtain hopefully very reliable end-user behavior results, they sometimes will incur the cost of a real-world market test. There are several ways to do this. First, prototype products can be placed in their homes or places of business for a limited period of time, and they can then use the product for a while and then answer questions about the product suitability and their willingness-to-pay. Similarly, new services can be made available in a test situation for a limited period of time. Sometimes, at the end of the test period, the respondent is offered the opportunity to actually keep the product or service on a permanent basis, but usually they are told that they will be contacted later if the offering is eventually made available to the public. Often the respondents pay nothing for the new product or service during the test period, but this can vary - they might be given some kind of financial incentive to participate in the test, or they might even be required to pay something during the test. Secondly, market tests can take place in retail stores, and respondents are those who actually buy the product in the store, but then are stopped outside in the parking lot and thanked for their participation, and have to return the product, and are given a total cash refund plus an incentive on the spot, after a short interview session, or a follow-up appointment session.

Competitive Product or Service Interviewing: With today's rather invasive tracking of purchases is it easy to find out when somebody has made a purchase. For example, often when a person changes their auto or household insurance carrier, or changes their cell phone carrier, the carrier that lost the account will try to interview the person to find out why they switched carriers, and might even try to unhook the change with a special offer.

Research Via Observation: A qualitative method or learning about purchase or usage behavior is to observe buyers as they roam around a retail location or a shopping mall, or use a product in a *test kitchen* or a *test scenario* like using a power tool or repairing a car themselves. Of course this is done unobtrusively and without direct assistance to see if directions are adequate and followed properly, but then with follow-up questions after the observation session. For example, some buyers will be avid comparison shoppers while others will be very brand-specific and even very knowledgeable regarding features and price. Some buyers are today doing what is called "showrooming" in that they will go to a retail store to touch-and-feel a product, and ask many questions, but then go home and make a purchase online. Retailers are trying to defeat this behavior by offering online purchase coupled with in-store pickup that saves them time and shipping cost.

      Lastly, it is wise to consider a combination of market research modes for a particular project, often designated *multimode* research, and this should be addressed in the Market Research Planning phase that is identified in Figure 3. For example, for a new concept, often focus groups sessions are first conducted, and later a sequence of quanitative methods will be employed in order to do forecasts and eventually a business case.

60

2.4 THE OFFER PROFILE

In any market research, the product or service offer, or the operational or administrative change that is being researched must be clearly defined for the respondents. Obviously, they must know what they are evaluating, or else the results will be invalid. It should never be taken for granted that the respondents clearly know what they are responding to. In the psychology of interviewing or conducting focus groups, many persons will not admit that they do not understand the interviewer or moderator.

In this regard, we often first separate respondents into *"buyers"* and *"non-buyers"* by simply asking a question in this regard at the beginning of the session. For "buyers" it is good to follow up with brand-specific questions, and currently used apps and features. For example, if someone says that they have never bought or used a cell-phone, then a separate sequence of questions should be utilized. But if a respondent indicates a high degree of familiarity, then they should not be put though any "educational" questions on cell phone features and functions. If we are researching an entirely new concept, then it is still useful to ask if the respondent is at all familiar with the new concept, but still define the new concept so that there will be a uniform understanding of the concept across all respondents.

Often the term *"price-features-availability"* has been used as a shortcut to define the offer that is being researched. But the offer is more than this, and will involve many other explicit and implicit elements. Some respondents will be very brand-conscious and will pay more for a trusted brand, and others don't care about brand identification and even like the idea of a new brand if the features and price are right. Some consumer respondents will shop only at familiar retail locations, and some factory buyers will purchase only through familiar suppliers and subcontractors. And some respondents will be more sensitive than others regarding things like warranty, return policy, couponing, senior discounts, and so forth. These factors go beyond the narrow price-features definition of a product or service.

The following is a list of some of the more important items to be considered in the Offer Profile when planning market research.

Offer Profile Checklist

Features and Functions: What does the product or service that is being researched do for the end user? What is standard and what is optional?

APPS: If the offer includes software features, are there "apps" available to add additional functionality, and if so, what are these apps and how are they available.

Third-Party Features and Functions: If available, can the buyer have other features or functions included either later or at point of sale, which are provided separate from the selling entity?

Pricing Plan: How can the buyer pay for the product or service that is being redearched, namely one-time payment, subscription, contract terms, extended payment, rent, buy or lease, credit cards accepted, prepayment penalty, early contract termination fees, etc.?

Trade-Ins: Will trade-ins be offered for this product or service, and if so what are the terms and conditions for trade-ins?

Pricing Level: Actual cost(s) to the buyer, in local currency, including quantity discounts, cash discounts, etc.

Warranty: What, if any, warranty terms are part of the offering being researched?

Return Policy: Can the item being researched be returned and if so what is the timing and money-back policy.

Brand Identification of the Product or Service: What is the branding for the offer being researched.

Association Discounts: As part of the offer, is there any discount for AAA, AARP, veterans, or any other group?

Senior Discount: Is there any discount for buyers over the age of 65 or any other age?

Couponing: Is there any manufacturer's coupon available for this offer?

Buying Location(s): **Where can the buyer find and complete a transaction for purchase of this product or service?**

Online Purchase or Manufacturer/Originator Website: **At which, if any, websites can the prospective buyer obtain this product or service?**

Co-Marketing Deals: **If known at the time of researching, or if it is part of the research and product planning, will there be any co-marketing deals with other manufacturers or retailers?**

Merchandising Environment: **Will there be any planned merchandising deals for this product or service, either at the wholesale, distributor or retailer levels?**

Finally, regarding the above discussion of the "Offer Profile," remember that all respondents behave differently, and some will be highly sensitive to certain elements of the product or service offer, and some respondents will have little or no concern for some of the above items.

2.5 QUESTIONAIRE DESIGN & TESTING

One way to start planning a specific market research project is to collect raw questions that need to be answered. But remember that this raw question list is far from the final questions that will be included in the actual executed research, whether it be qualitative or quantitative in nature. This collection of raw questions can be done

(securely) with an email broadcast (encrypted) to a list of stakeholders and prior team participants, or merely to the heads of organizations for which you would like assess their needs, for the coming quarter or coming year. But often it is good to start collecting questions when the initial information team sessions are conducted, and to keep improving on the list of raw questions as the overall process proceeds. Of course, at some point, the final information needs must be frozen with total buy-in on the part of all stakeholders and sponsors.

Such a survey of in-house research needs should be done carefully. You do not want to commit to obtaining some information before the overall research needs are assessed and prioritized.

Once a long list of questions are collected in this raw form, it is a very important task to carefully begin to formulate actual questions and build a draft questionnaire. This is where experience and knowledge come into play. If survey questions are scripted and presented improperly and in the incorrect sequence, the research results will be compromised or even entirely invalid for further forecasting and analysis. It is a good idea to circulate drafts to obtain buy-in, and it is also a good idea to actually test out a questionnaire either in-house or on test respondents (online or face-to-face) before going-live and fully launching the execution of a market research project.

Also, even before execution, it is a good idea to lay out a research analysis program that is specific to the particular research being conducted, plus the corresponding modeling environment. Then, when the results are obtained, you can immediately begin analysis and forecasting.

Demographic Profile Questions

Every market research session must begin with demographic *identification* of who is being interviewed. For online Panels, most of this demographic profile information will have been collected when the respondents signed up to participate in the Panel, but often additional demographic information needs to be obtained that is specific to the product or service targeting for the research project that is being conducted. For mall-intercept or telephone interviews or other face-to-face research modes, the respondent will usually be totally new and unidentified, so they need to be profiled before any actual product or service research questions are posed.

Demographic Profile Questions should be completely separated from the main research, and should be done in private. The name and address of the participant need not be explicitly identified, but at least a telephone number or web address should be obtained, since this will be needed for verification of the research session on a spot-check basis. Care should be taken to minimize any invasive aspects, especially with today's security concerns. If the up-front demographic profile session is not complete, then the session should not proceed further, since the product-service responses will be useless in terms of eventual cell weighting, forecasting, and modeling.

For online panels, the software should be designed to indicate that the demographic questions are mandatory, and the respondent should be blocked from going further in the self-administered online session until all necessary demographic questions are properly answered.

Sensitive personal demographic cell identification should be via *age ranges, income ranges,* and so forth, so that respondents are not forced to explicitly state their age or personal income directly. Both open-ended unaided and multiple-choice aided questions should be included as check points.

There should be at least one or two *additional check questions* in the demographic session to assure valid responses. For example, when youth or tween or teenage respondents are interviewed, they might respond to some questions with nonsensical answers, and this will usually invalidate the entire session.

Up-Front Respondent Assurances and Disclaimers

Respondents should acknowledge understanding of a well-stated legal disclaimer that they will not reveal or misrepresent anything in the survey session, that their answers are sincere and correct and forthright to the best of their ability, and that they will not do anything of a non-competitive nature if there is branding identification in the session. These statements should be reviewed for legal completeness and validity by the sponsoring organization, but should not scare the respondent or inhibit answers in the survey. (Be aware that some persons are litigation-focused and will try to make false claims against an entity about fictitious damages.) Further, the respondents should be assured that there is nothing in the survey session of a sales-pitch nature and that the information that they provide will be held in strict confidence and that nothing is ever sold or provided to any third parties. If respondents fail to certify these statements, they should not go further in the survey.

Discrete and Redundant Coding of Questionnaires

For identification, questionnaires, either via Panels, via telephone, face-to-face, or otherwise should be coded in a discrete and redundant fashion to make sure that responses can be identified properly and associated with demographic and verification information.

Questioning Sequence

The proper sequencing of survey questions is very important. We do not not want to "spoil the session" with an improper sequencing of questions. Often the order of questions is varied in "rotation groups" to try to eliminate any sequence bias. The offer statement itself must be user-friendly and up front in the survey, before any further details. Features and functions should be clear and include a *needs example* to aid the respondent but not lead any of their responses and not put "words in their mouth." It is good to put up front some questions regarding the persona and decision psychology of the respondent, but in a discrete and non-invasive manner, in order to identify what type of buyer or non-buyer is being interviewed. The order of questions is paramount. Pricing plans and price information should come well after an understanding of the "total offer" that includes things like warranty, availability, and the Offer Profile statements that were delineated in the previous section above. Respondents want to please the interviewer and can lie and misrepresent themselves somewhat, and there should be several check questions to address the consistency and sincerity of their responses. The questionnaire sequence should recognize that for some respondents, even one negative association with the offer can then influence their further responses in the survey. For example, even if a respondent likes the features and functions, but they do not like the sales conditions or warranty or return policy, that this can influence their purchase intent responses that follow.

Price Levels and Pricing Plans

Several price points should always be offered and stated in price ranges, so that a price-demand relationship can be constructed. Since price is important, at least one check question should be included regarding price. It should be arranged that pricing plan responses can be separated from price level responses. For example, some respondents might have a reasonable willingness-to-pay but not like any of the pricing plans associated with the offer statement in the survey.

Needs and Wants

Some surveys deal with offers that are purely discretionary purchases, and other surveys deal with fundamental needs and even life-threatening situations. This should be recognized in the survey accordingly. However, willingness-to-pay does not always logically follow needs-and-wants since self-esteem and buyer psychology will strongly influence purchase intent.

Purchase Environment Simulation

A market research session is trying to simulate the actual purchase environment, including all of the factors associated with branding and merchandising. The respondent should be put in the correct frame of mind in this regard, as much as possible, but without any sales-pitch connotations.

Finally, here are some steps to be followed in questionnaire design:

1. FIRST, lay out all of the demographic cells indicated by the targeting and segmentation plan for the offering, as determined by the Research Planning and other tasks that were identified in the integrated process of Figure 3.

2. SECONDLY, lay out the complete Offer Profile, including which elements will be important items in the modeling, forecasting and sensitivity analysis which will follow. Make sure that the question

70

sequence is logical and does not force the respondent into any situation where they will answer a question merely to be consistent but not convey their true feelings and intentions.

3. THIRD, include Buyer and Non-Buyer sections such that there are "skip-arounds" in the survey to avoid unnecessary questions for knowledgeable buyers. Also at this point, formulate Check Questions to weed-out nonsensical and inconsistent responses.

4. FOURTH, for both online self-administered panels, and for scripted telephone and face-to-face interviews, review and proof-read everything, and keep track of the survey overall timing so that completions will be high.

5. FIFTH AND FINALLY, the questionnaire must be *tested*, both in-house and then in a few test sessions with real test respondents who do not know that this is a test. After testing, corrections should be made to the questionnaire as needed.

2.6 SAMPLING MARKET RESEARCH RESPONDENTS

Sampling analysis begins with determination of the demographic cells which must be projected and modeled. A *cell* means a group determined by age, income, occupation, sex, and other basic data. For each of these cells, statistical significance must be attained, and sparseness must be avoided. Our objective is to

71

generalize the results of the market research to the targeted segments, not the general population. It is usually assumed that sampling will be *random*, meaning that there is no bias in the sampling procedure of the market research. For example, that for the chosen cell, a spread across the demographic variables will not exclude any group, like those who work versus those not working, or those of a particular religion, versus those of another religion or cultural background, and so forth. Also, it must be assumed that the interest level for a particular offering is large compared to the targeted population, such that the offering is not so peculiar that very few would be at all interested out of the entire targeted population.

For each of the cells, we need to establish a *"confidence percentage level,"* which usually is 95%, and a confidence interval. Then, assuming randomness, the sample size can be calculated. There are many online sources for doing this calculation, or you can download software and do the calculation locally. You can also delve further into statistical testing algorithms and procedures if you like, and again many references exist for doing this further analysis. One main point to emphasize is that since there are so many *"extraneous variables"* like the respondent's race and ethnic origin, their birthplace, the size of the respondent's family, the size of his/her place of dwelling and owned or rented, their physical size and weight characteristics, their diet and nutrition, their clothing style, their IQ and EQ, their material possessions, their hobbies and sports, what they watch on TV, what they browse on the Internet, and on-and-on, that one cannot possibly assure a random sample across the extraneous variables. But what we can do, and must do, is use experience and judgment to try to eliminate bias in the sampling. For example, if anything having to do with automobiles is being researched, and that targeting and segmentation is focused on automobile purchase, such as brand preference, brand loyalty, purchase or lease habits, price-demand, etc., that it is very important to include questions in the demographic profiling and also in the main survey to make sure that there is no bias in the sample toward one brand or one purchase mode, regarding automobiles, and that everything else in the sample will be assumed to be random. This requires both knowledge, judgment, and experience on the part of the researcher and collectively on the part of the Research Team. This aspect of sampling for market research is more of an art than a statistical sampling calculation.

In a Panel, the participants are pre-certified according to a wide range of demographic variables, but after a final and complete targeting and segmentation plan has been established, it might be necessary to further survey the Panelists on additional demographic and profiling variables prior to selecting the actual sample for a particular research project. This will help remove any bias that is associated with the targeting and segmentation, from the Panel market research that is being conducted.

In mall-intercept recruitment of respondents, the supplier's agents roam the mall looking for persons who appear to fit the cells that are segmented and targeted for the particular market research project. The supplier's agents need to be well-trained to do this task, since the demographic assessment questions at the start of the session might not filter across all variables.

In telephone call-out research, respondents are often selected by zip code and then telephone exchange. Sometimes a pre-call list of prospective respondents has been compiled from other sources, like web-access and search engine data, point-of-purchase data (obtained via retailer discount card databases and credit card databases). Random calling of numbers is much less efficient and will be considered invasive by many answering parties, and can start off an interview session in a negative manner.

Mailed-out paper surveys and email surveys give the receiving parties the option of participation or not, so they feel more in control of the interview process, and are likely to start the survey in a more positive manner.

Purchase survey cards and optional post-purchase surveys again allow the prospective respondents to participate or not, so they are in control and are more likely to feel positive about the interview. Those who have had a very positive experience and will give a glowing review, plus those who have had a negative experience and wish to register complaints often dominate this type of post-purchase survey. Those in the middle are likely to never respond.

Finally, selection of respondents is both a science and an art. An experienced research organization will have a proven track record that can be verified with references and testimonials. Often the primary research supplier will subcontract elements of the overall research project, including recruitment and screening of respondents. It is an important element of the Market Research Plan to review all recruitment and sampling activities.

2.7 FIELDING & EXECUTING MARKET RESEARCH

After the proper preparation and planning, a market research program will commence with the actual interviews and data collection. This is where the "rubber hits the road" and it is too late to fiddle with the questionnaires and sampling, targeting, segmentation, and respondent recruitment process. Therefore, it is mandatory that all steps in the Research Plan be thoroughly reviewed, with buy-in obtained by all stakeholders, before "pressing the button" to execute the research.

For an Online Panel, this execution phase can be quite rapid, and data collection can be fully automated and mechanized, with raw report generation almost instantaneous. In fact, research sponsors can often be securely linked directly into the Panel platform servers, and observe the collection of results in real time.

In the case of Focus Groups, the observing sponsors can stop the session if it is not going right, for example if one of the participants is spoiling or warping the session. This can be done by a discrete real-time phone call directly to the focus group moderator, to please stop the session and excuse the misbehaving participant.

Similarly, with real-time monitoring of progress for a Panel, sponsors can interrupt the survey if something is going wrong, and then continue with the online panel after any required fix. Of course, any interrupted results might not be valid and need to be checked carefully.

Once a Mailer Survey or a Broadcast Email type of survey is sent out, if errors are found, retraction can be damaging to the interview process, and so it is likely that an entirely new list of prospective respondents needs to be selected.

Trying to stop Mall-Intercept can be very expensive, and can interrupt the research schedule quite a bit, since the interviewing facility is often booked far in advance.

Interrupting a session of invited-in senior executives (as well as busy managers like production managers, financial managers, supply chain managers, etc.) can be particularly damaging and rescheduling of their time slots can face severe problems and delays.

So the above issues regarding interrupting a survey that has begun execution should indicate to the reader that it is highly important to review everything and run test interviews prior to actually initiating any market research.

Research Venue and Location Considerations

For Mall-Intercept and any invited-in Focus Groups or face-to-face live interviewing, the location of the sessions must be carefully selected. Locations should fit the targeting and segmentation cells, and this can be analyzed using the many Zip-Code databases. Unfortunately, sometimes those executing a market research program will choose locations based on their own convenience or familiarity, and of course this could introduce a bias factor.

Live Interviewer or Moderator Persona Considerations

The personality, vocal characteristics, and behavior of the Focus Group Moderator or the live telephone Interviewer is critical, and can affect the responses of the research participants. The sex, professional demeanor, and vocabulary (research subject terminology and pronunciation) is important, and must properly fit the target segments being interviewed. If the moderator or face-to-face or telephone interviewed does not exhibit the correct vocal behavior, body-language, and appearance, then research results will be affected. Of course, in the case of a self-administered Online Panel, there are no such issues. Training of the moderators and interviewers should include proper screening and discussion of the psychology of the interviewing process.

2.8 ANALYZING MARKET RESEARCH

Once market research results are available, it is

77

necessary to follow a disciplined series of steps to validate the results and begin analysis of the findings. Sometimes eager sponsors will get hold of the initial raw results and begin to announce findings or make statements prematurely. So the research program needs to have a strict "need-to-know" security and information control process built into the process.

The first thing to do before any actual analysis is undertaken is to identify and discard the following in a *"Cleansing Task"* which removes the following types of responses:

- **Partial or Incomplete Results** *(the respondent dropped out of the survey prematurely for a variety of reasons)*

- **Inconsistent Results** *(respondents who did not correctly and consistently complete the included check questions)*

- **Nonsensical Results** *(on open-ended questions, respondents provided illogical or "wise-guy" responses)*

Secondly, the raw results must be *weighted* according to a demographic scheme that was previously established in the Market Research Plan, as indicated in Figure 3. Usually age and income cells are the first items for which weighting is applied. Of course, the targeting and segmentation plan for this research program are the base to be weighted against, rather than demographics of the general population. For example, if the targeted segment for the research is factory buyers of both sexes in a particular industry, the weighting should bring the survey sample in line with the exact statistics of this target group. The raw data will show some under-representation or over-representation compared to the exact targeted group demographics, and the difference is the weighting correction that must be applied. Of course, weighting need not be this simple, and could be a more complex multivariable function, and even have a temporal dimension.

Once market research data is: (1) Cleansed, and (2) Weighted, then analysis of the results can begin. Be aware that if Cleansing reveals many gross errors, or Weighting reveals a flawed survey sample, then the whole fielding and execution of the market research might have to be redone, but this is the extreme case.

Tabulation reports are first prepared on a question-by-question basis, and then some *Cross-Tabs* can be prepared. For example, of those who had a high purchase intent, what was their preference for the type of supply channel? Or, how do "buyers" and "non-buyers" compare across all questions or in regard to certain critical questions? However, in doing cross-tabs, always be aware that there might be sparseness in a particular cell and therefore the cross-tabulation should merely be considered a qualitative indicator and not statistically significant.

When analyzing market research results, make sure

that a logical and disciplined parsing of responses is maintained. Don't jump around, and try to separate groups of responses clearly. There is no hard-and-fast rule in doing this, so the experience and skill of the research supplier, the sponsor, and the market research team in general are important in tailoring the analysis of the results to the particular project and industry.

Finally, it will come time for the market research results to be formally presented to the Research Team and eventually to certain key stakeholders and executives. Confidentiality and security is highly important in doing this, and reports should be numbered and online access doubly password protected, and the "need to know" rule strictly applied. Competitors will be eager to get hold of your data and reports. Also, keep good records, and don't throw away anything arbitrarily, and have a strict research retention policy.

2.9 USES OF SECONDARY RESEARCH

A basic rule in market research is to never repeat something that has recently already been done. The Research Audit Phase of the Integrated Research Process (Figure 3) should always be one of the tasks completed before planning new research. A second rule in research is to fit the problem. If some recent and still valid Secondary Research, typically a multiclient study or a speculative independent study, is available, it should be thoroughly reviewed and analyzed and the authors and sponsoring entity should be contacted for a discussion.

Sometimes, if a *market potential estimate* will be suitable for an early business case or an *investment-spending decision* then this information should be presented to the Research Team and the sponsors, to see if such secondary research information is sufficient for total buy-in to proceed. Sometimes secondary research is sufficient to initiate a project, pending the next *Phase Review* of a multi-phase program, and eventually fully quantitative primary market research will be conducted later when the initiative proceeds to later Phases in a *Phased-Development Process*.

If validated and reviewed and authored from a trusted source, secondary market research can be valuable in determining technical, market, cultural, economic, regulatory, and competitive trends.

2.10 DATA MINING

Today there is so much data that is available online that it is important to have a very specific plan to conduct "Data Mining" and to make sure that it does not take on a life of its own.

Start any data mining with the most fundamental and authoritative sources. Avoid "one-off" reports and purely academic or student reports.

Appendix B lists some of the many *Secondary Research and Data Mining* sources that are available. One of the most fundamental of these is the BEA (Bureau of

Economic Analysis) in the U.S. Dept. of Commerce, and the data are *free and online*. They collect and interpret and project data from many sources and this information can be used to start targeting and segmentation tasks and to set up the *forecast base* needed for modeling and forecasting. Some of this data is stated right down to the county and Zip Code level if you need to get that detailed. Also, the Census Bureau in the U.S. Dept. of Commerce is responsible for the 10-year U.S. Census, and also produces interim reports.

You might have your favorite sources if you are working within a particular industry, but always make sure of the sources and reliability and keep good records for your later reference. Avoid any industry *hearsay* and don't let the "crowd effect" influence your own judgment.

While doing data mining and reviewing secondary research, at the same time collect competitive information, or at least the most reliable sources, but again do not let competitive data or analysis of such take on a life of its own. Your main focus is the particular project here-and-now, and competitive information often has a substantial time lag associated with it, and of course the real strategies of competitors are not in the public domain and they might even leak incorrect information to derail their own competitors.

2.11 MARKET RESEARCH SOFTWARE AVAILABLE

If you retain a well established and reliable market

research supplier, they will have their own favorite software platforms (usually licensed from an IT developer), and you will then be concerned with the output and not the software itself. But if you want to conduct research and analysis in-house, then it is good to keep up with the software available.

Appendix C lists some of the many, but certainly not all, sources for software that will support and aid market research, forecasting, & business case development. You should always fully test any software before using it, if you have not applied this version of the software previously, and usually the software vendor will let you do such testing free of charge. Also, you should check on reviews and testimonials, and talk to other users about their own experiences with the software package. Be careful of any online reviews - sometimes these are fake reviews that are written by proxy names assumed by the IT developer themselves.

2.12 CLOUD COMPUTING VERSUS IN-HOUSE SERVERS

If you contract with an outside market research supplier, they automatically will become a "cloud computing" platform as far as your research data and analysis is concerned. You can request a mirror-copy of everything downloaded to your own in-house servers, for backup and later reference, but the research supplier (and their subcontractors and outsourcing and offshoring partners) will have copies of your proprietary research data. And regarding downloading and-or back-and-forth access to the suppliers servers, make sure that the networking is highly secure, and usually via a VPN (virtual private network) rather than via the public Internet without encryption. Also, make sure that you have non-compete and security agreements in place. Another reason for having your own copy of everything is that if you switch market research suppliers, you will want to be able to access any past information without having to go back to a research supplier and pay for the old data.

Maintaining in-house servers for everything you do is very expensive, and of course you must have a complete support and maintenance staff to do this. Otherwise, you will be bringing in outside IT vendors every time you have a problem or need to make updates and changes, and such vendors will then have access to virtually all of your research data and need to sign security agreements themselves.

In today's rich and sometimes confusing online computing environment, keeping up with the IT housekeeping aspects of market research and analysis is an important task. Make sure that you do not fall into a false sense of security regarding competitive analysis and security and hacking threats.

*****

PART THREE

MODELING AND FORECASTING

3.1 FORECASTING FROM MARKET RESEARCH

For many forecasting projects, the best way to determine demand is to ask customers and-or others relevant to the matter. As discussed previously, however obvious this is, many "forecasting" organizations focus first on historical legacy information and statistical analysis, and then try "judgmental" methods but totally exclude modeling and market research from their forecasting methodologies.

Market research in its broadest sense includes secondary research, data mining, and primary research. Usually, research that has already been done is evaluated first, as well as data mining of many governmental, trade group, and industrial sources of information. Some secondary research organizations specialize in particular areas, such as technical innovation, software and computer systems, drugs and pharmaceuticals, natural resources, medical advances, and so forth, and they publish their own reports that keep up with the latest trends and market potential areas. Such secondary research sources can be invaluable for exploring new opportunities and supporting any decision-making process. Likewise, many governmental and trade data sources that are uncovered through data mining are often free and can provide a solid basis for planning any further research or forecasting.

Primary research can cover respondents who are either the actual end-user consumers, but also might be industrial and supply-chain buyers, as well as many other individuals and entities. These could be those involved in R&D, those in the production cycle, operational and administrative individuals, and those in the supply chain. Sometimes research will include investors and venture capital groups, regulators, governmental entities, expert consultants, and academics.

Whatever the definition and scope of primary research respondents, there are a number of rules and steps which must be followed, regardless of the target segments or scope of the research.

The business model of an entity might not involve any direct end-user contact at all, but ultimately the financial results of the entity will depend on demand for the offering. Even a holding company's success is ultimately linked to the financial results of the operating entities in which it has invested, and these operational enterprises either sell directly to end-users or to other enterprises which supply equipment and services to other enterprises that ultimately serve end-users. That is why many models of the economy state that eventually the "consumer market" drives macroeconomic results.

This Part Three focuses on modeling and

forecasting based on both *primary* market research and *secondary* market research. Secondary research and related data mining are usually used for *market potential* forecasting as opposed to direct demand forecasting, and can guide a "back of the envelope" business case to get started, as long as this secondary research is up to date and directly relevant. In the modeling and forecasting discussion in this book, the focus is microeconomic demand, and macroeconomic factors are beyond consideration or overlayed in the forecast assumptions.

3.2 CONCEPTUALIZATION

The process of constructing a marketplace or operational model that will be used for forecasting and simulation begins with conceptualization, as has been mentioned in previous Sections. We must not only define the problem and its analysis, but also the total context, and the goals and objectives. The development of the model should be conducted before planning any market research that might be needed, because research is but one of the activities for generating data to populate and run the model.

This conceptualization of the problem and the proper model might seem unnecessary to some. Most forecasting analysts want to jump right in and would claim that of course we know the problem - *"let's do a forecast and get started right away."* They want to start plugging in numbers to some software to see what kind of results they get. In cases like this, the "garbage in, garbage out" rule dominates.

87

But conceptualization of the forecast problem and process in the beginning of a program eventually pays back big with a quality forecast and a model that permits sensitivity analysis and simulation. We need to start off with questions like: "Who needs the forecast and when do they need it and for what time frame into the future? " "Is the product or service or concept to be forecasted already fully defined or still in concept or prototype stage?" " Do product development or technical groups want different forecasts so that they can set priorities for features and functions that they might develop?" "Or do advertising and promotion organizations want to know the forecasted sensitivity to their possible program themes and targeted market segments before they commit to such programs?"

Maybe it is not a sales forecast at all that is needed, but rather a forecast of changes in attitudes toward a product or service. Or maybe it is a forecast of evolution in buying behavior for the channel mix, such as migration from in-store to online buying, or knowing the prevalence of in-store "showrooming" and then buying online with a better deal.

Conceptualization can either be done by one individual who will be generating a forecast, or by a small knowledgeable team that is highly compatible and cooperative, composed of people who can work together on defining what is needed to be forecasted plus all of the factors for which the forecasting process must account.

3.3 THE FORECAST BASE

Except for a few rare cases, we never want to forecast demand or opinions or any research responses to the entire population. In other words, every Market Research Plan will automatically be associated with a *targeting and segmentation plan* for the offering or the fundamental project goals and objectives. But the forecast base might not always be the same as the targeted and segmented cells. For example, in the Market Research Plan, we might want to survey beyond the targeted and segmented cells, to see if there are buyers and non-buyers that we have not been targeting, but then, to be conservative, we might confine the forecast to a subset of those surveyed. Or, we might be surprised by the market research findings, and then decide to expand the forecast base to other cells.

This book is primarily focused on forecasts based on market and strategic models. The market side of modeling should always be based primarily on market research findings, but sometimes we might want to "seed" the model with historical trend data for previous buyers, if we make an assumption that previous buyers will find a new offering attractive, and that this assumption is supported by the market research findings for the buyer portion of the results. But always remember that the statistical trend can be incorrect if any of the total offering factors, like price level and pricing plans, advertising, promotion, supply chain, and merchandising have changed from what was in place in the past for previous buyers of a similar offering.

Also, the forecast base should take into account fundamental demographic changes, such as those that are identified in Census and DEA data and projections of these data.

3.4 BASIC AND EXTENDED FORECASTING MODELS

To illustrate what is meant by a forecasting model, consider again Figure 1, repeated below, which depicts the basic demand forecasting model for marketing a product or service through a channel mix.   This is a "causal" model in general forecasting terms, but is the only type of

FIGURE 1 (repeated)

THE MOST BASIC FORECAST MODEL

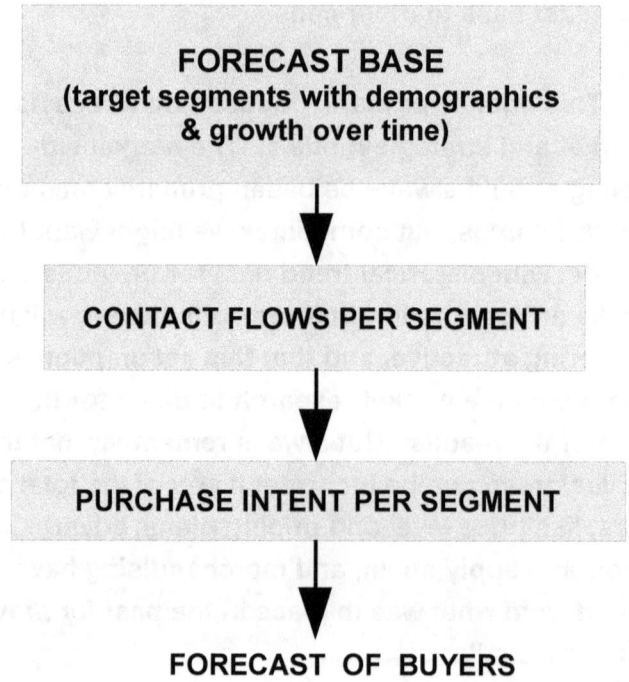

FORECAST BASE
(target segments with demographics
& growth over time)

CONTACT FLOWS PER SEGMENT

PURCHASE INTENT PER SEGMENT

FORECAST OF BUYERS

direct forecasting model which captures the realities of here-and-now versus statistical legacy trending.

This model simply states that when purchase intent is obtained through market research, that in order to obtain a forecast for this, the purchase intent needs to be applied to a flow of buyer contacts. called "contact flows" in the second diagram box.

The steps in this simple illustrative model are as follows:

1. Start with a *"Forecast Base"* of households or decision-makers or organizational entities, covering all targeted segments. This could be set up as a "pull through" model, in which the targets are end-users, or a "push-through" model in which the targets are elements of the supply chain, like wholesalers, distributors, and retailers. Obviously, any market research being forecasted must have included these chosen target segments, however defined. For example, survey samples of end-users should always obtain age, income, education, and occupation demographics, if not many other survey questions about lifestyle, product and service usage, etc. This applies to existing panels that are kept current, as well as any custom primary research.

2. Then develop *"Contact Flows"* for these segments. An end-user contact could be generated because of a lifecycle change (such as a birth, death, divorce,

91

marriage) , a physical household change (move, new household formation, major remodeling), an educational change (graduation, starting school), a health change (medical diagnosis, insurance change, accident), a financial change (new job, job change, promotion, layoff, inheritance, financial loss), maintenance of equipment (breakage, failures, ageing), response to a number of promotion and advertising programs (TV, print, online, web searches), and general buyer stimulation (hearsay, personal psychology). A supply chain push-though contact could be generated by a periodic sales call, by response to an offer like a new volume discount, by trade-show activities, and so forth.

3. Third in the simple Basic Model of the above figure, we apply *Purchase Intent* obtained from market research (panels, secondary, or primary research in many modes), making sure that this purchase intent is closely matched to the segment flow demographics (price point, timing, etc.), and also only the purchase intent for your own particular brand, so that you take into account competition and market share.

4. The result is a forecast of buying behavior for this product or service, for the time period(s) that match the segment contact flows.

Of course, things are not this simple in the real world, but the above Figure 1 model illustrates a number of points. First, when conceptualizing and planning market research and forecasting, it is important to start with a universe and then a forecast base of potential targeted buyers and non-buyers. Do not assume that everybody will buy the product or service, but neither should it be assumed that existing buyers are the only target segments, since non-buyers and brand-switchers could be a significant group. Secondly, throughout any modeling, it is important to make sure that all elements and assumptions are orchestrated and synchronized. Price points and features that are stated in market research must match actual sales contacts and merchandising and promotion and advertising, or else the resulting forecast will be invalid.

But now let us consider a more developed and realistic forecast model, which is primarily for a packaged-goods type of product in the consumer market, but designated here as *"An Extended Basic Forecast Model."* Usually we need a forecast model which incorporates assumptions on price, advertising, promotion, the supply chain, retailing and merchandising, and buyer psychology. So, for further illustration of the modeling process, consider now the Extended Model depicted in Figure 4 on the next page.

FIGURE 4

ENHANCED FORECAST MODEL
(PACKAGED GOODS)

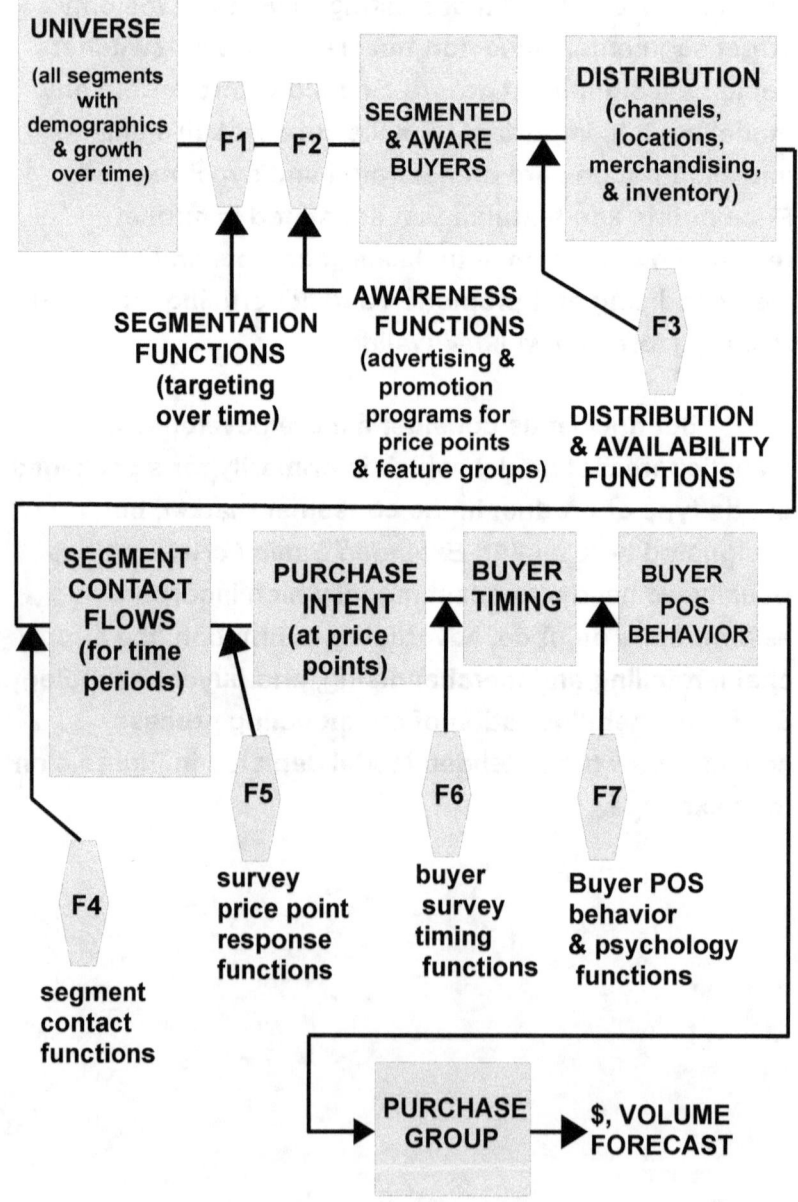

In this extended model example, a number of things have been added, to get closer to the reality of the market environment. Again, this generalized "extended basic model" is focused around a packaged-goods type of opportunity. So, this particular model is for a product or service that is offered through retail channels, be it online or at brick-and-mortar locations. The "Functions" which have been added, namely F1 through F7, now incorporate assumptions about important elements in the marketing chain. By definition, these are:

Universe = The full demographic base against which the forecast is being developed. This base is end-user segments categorized according to many specific data elements, starting with age, income, occupation, and education, but also including past buying behavior, buying habits, attitude, and many other segmentation parameters. This data will vary over time, as buyer generations change, and is obtained via panels, secondary research, and is also obtained in the specific primary research for the forecast to be synchronized with the marketing program schedule.

F1 = *Segmentation Functions,* the demographic segments for which this product or service is actually targeted, and these segments might vary over time, as a product rollout proceeds and the product and its features and functions mature over its product lifecycle. The F1 Functions permit forecast sensitivity and simulation as targeting assumptions vary.

F2 = *Awareness Functions,* the results of advertising and

95

promotion programs for this product, as they might vary over the lifecycle. The F2 Functions typically will be the variation in exposure per advertising or promotion dollar. The F2 Functions permit forecast sensitivity and simulation as advertising and promotion dollars vary. For example an F2 Function could be a curve or table or formula relating an awareness percentage to dollars spent, as indicated below.

This kind of Awareness Factor would be generated for each channel in the targeted channel mix of the product or service program, but would still be a function of the awareness dollars allocated. An example of an Awareness Factor function is indicated below.

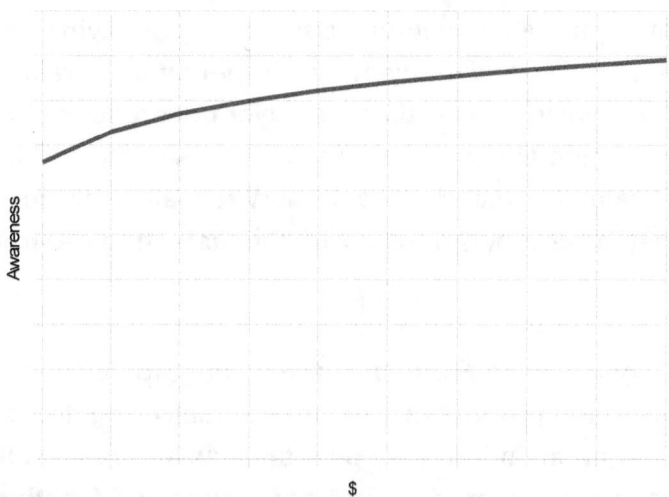

$A = A_0 + ((x+1)^{(1-n)} -1)/(1-n)$

A=Awareness

A_0=Awareness at zero dollars, due to merchandising

x=Awareness dollars

n=Awareness curve shape factor

This is just a single curve representation of awareness, and indicates the general diminishing returns of advertising, and also has a latent awareness at zero advertising, which of course is both a function of time, brand equity, and brand loyalty. In a fully developed demand model, awareness could be a much more complicated function of advertising, promotion, targeted audience, advertising media mix, viewer retention, prior brand stimulation, and so forth. With a much more complicated awareness function, input variables to the forecast model can be expanded in order to run sensitivity analysis.

Continuing with definitions for the Functions in the above model diagram:

F3 = *Distribution & Availability Functions*, which capture the channel mix assumptions. The product rollout and lifecycle management might begin with an introduction in certain channels, and later expand to all channels or to a different mix of channels, as appropriate to market response, retail merchandising programs, production and inventory capabilities. For example, a geographic market coverage Distribution Factor could be created that is a function of retail locations. And a related Availability Factor could be created which accounts for store merchandising. Of course, for the *online distribution channel*, distribution and availability are essentially 100%, except for possible shipping restrictions. For distribution via telephone sales, as a toll-free number advertised on TV, distribution again is essentially high, but with perhaps some limitations on the inbound toll-free call center scripting and order-taking and fulfillment process.

F4 = *Segment Contact Functions*, for each of the segments that have been selected and targeted to a distribution mix, what are the Segment Contact Functions that will actually drive buyers to these channels? These Functions are beyond the Awareness advertising and promotion programs, and include specific ways to create sales contacts. These programs will include specific online, in-store, mailer, catalog, couponing, co-marketing, TV, mobile, and other specific programs. The inputs are typically dollars spent, so that forecast sensitivity and simulation can be run for various Contact campaigns. For example, for a TV toll-free response channel, what % of the viewing audience is actually applicable for contact? And for online users, what % who are made aware will actually respond to an online program and make contact.

F5 = *Purchase Intent Functions*, which are obtained via market research, either secondary or primary, using whatever research modes are selected. These are brand-specific, so that this is where competitive market share is taken into account, for a particular price. and pricing plan. These Functions might include a degree of complexity to account for the fact that as pricing and pricing plans might vary, buyers might switch brands and therefore the forecast market share will vary. This type of data is obtained in a variety of market research modes. Sometimes buyer-simulation trials are conducted in actual brick-and-mortar stores to test purchase intent, but often purchase intent is obtained via self-report in a face-to-face or online or telephone survey. The research data obtained should have explored price and pricing plans and brand preferences, so that forecast sensitivity and simulations can generate different forecasts for various prices and pricing plans.

F6 = *Buyer Timing Functions*, which account for the fact that buyers do not always intend to purchase immediately, but in research often indicate when they will intend to buy. For example, do they intend to buy a new house or a new car within a few months or within the next year. These functions should be included in a model to make sure that purchase intent is not incorrectly credited to the wrong forecast time slot.

F7 = *Buyer POS Behavior Functions* are included to account for the buyer psychology and persona at point of contact. Well-meaning and motivated buyers all have different personal decision processes. Many need to consult with a spouse or friends or families before making a major purchase. And some are impulse buyers who will not comparison shop and can be brought to closing on a purchase at the first contact. F7 is a correction factor and permits sensitivity assumptions to be simulated.

The flow in above Figure 4 and the above definitions of the Functions F1 through F7 will provide the reader with an idea of the important elements that need to be incorporated in a Model which is needed to convert market research into actual forecasts. This is merely a generalized example, primarily for the demand of a product or service targeted to the consumer market, and it is *mandatory* that you always develop your own models for your particular offering, industry, and operations. Don't just plan to plug in numbers to somebody else's model for a different offering.

3.5 EXAMPLE MODELS FOR VARIOUS INDUSTRIES

For particular offerings, models need to be developed that fit the marketplace and operational environment, but as a guideline, could follow the format similar to that indicated in the Figure 4 discussion. However, it is paramount to know the particular industry statistics before modeling and forecasting, so the *Integrated Process* of Figure 3 must be applied for the particular project.

There are many market research suppliers who specialize in certain industries, like pharmaceuticals, travel, hotel-motel, energy, communications, high-tech, government, defense, apparel, and so forth. They should be consulted for assistance and ideas in building new forecast models, planning and analyzing market research, and at least in reviewing what you develop in-house.

But again, an important prerequisite for any modeling is an understanding of the industry statistics. For example, trying to model and forecast a particular automobile brand without knowing about the global auto industry will result in an incomplete model and forecast errors. Trends like hybrid and electric cars, online auto configuration before buying, auto purchase financing trends, and so forth are among the many key factors that must be taken into account when modeling and forecasting a particular automobile demand. Just trending past auto buying statistics can lead to incorrect conclusions regarding the future.

Here are several important steps to follow in building a particular industry and brand model.

(1) KNOW THE INDUSTRY, NOT JUST YOUR BRAND *(Buyers switch brands and most markets today have a truly global infrastructure, so keep up with and subscribe to fundamental sources of data and industry trends. You need to know your company's operations but don't let this distract you from what is happening in the overall industry.)*

(2) BUILD BASIC MODELS AND THEN ADD SOPHISTICATION *(Don't try to include everything at once, but start your modeling with the basics of demand and decisions, and then add additional factors and corrections as you accumulate experience, knowledge, and skill at modeling and forecasting.)*

(3) LEARN FROM SUPPLIERS AND SOURCES, BUT BUILD YOU OWN CAPABILITIES *(Ask anybody about anything, but don't become codependent and helpless without the support of vendors and suppliers. You remain ultimately responsible.)*

To aid in the *industry-specifics* of model building, the following are some references in this regard.

(1) "Forecasting for the Pharmaceutical Industry,"

is a book by Arthur G. Cook, and is available for free download as a PDF file at
http://www.sadrabiotech.com/catalog/GOOD %20Forecasting%20for%20the%20Pharmaceutical %20Industry.pdf
This book has some useful ideas, but like many that you will come across, is based primarily on the same old statistical trending analysis perspective, which is applicable only if the past represents the future.

(2) *"Energy Forecasting and Modelling"* is an online PDF sales brochure from the French international consultants Enerdata, at
http://www.enerdata.net/brochure/Energy-forecasting-and-modelling-brochure.pdf and this brochure will give you ideas about modeling for the energy industry. Enerdata has many databases and publications applicable to the energy marketplace.

(4) "*Looking ahead: future market and business models*"
http://www.pwc.com/gx/en/utilities/ publications/assets/pwc-future-utility-business-models.pdf
This is a PWC (Price Waterhouse Coopers) PDF relating to eight possible future models for the energy industry.

(3) *Fashion United* *https://fashionunited.info* is a Dutch organization covering the global apparel industry.
"FashionUnited is an independent international

B2B fashion platform. Globally active, the website reaches more than 1.6 million industry professionals per month. At FashionUnited we strive for more fun and efficiency in fashion! That's why we created a one-stop-shop platform where visitors can find the latest fashion news, a career center, an events calendar, an article archive, various trade statistics, employer branding pages and more." Any modeling and forecasting of the apparel industry needs to start with an understanding of industry trends and activities. *https://fashionunited.info*

(4) *"Examples of business models from the music industry"*
https://www.boundless.com/users/235420/ textbooks/business-fundamentals/adding-products-and-services-13/adding-products-and-services-52/examples-of-business-models-from-the-music-industry-245-15548/ This is an educational website that describes eight business models in the music industry.

(5) *"Construction Trade Convergence"*
http://www.adlittle.com/downloads/tx_adlreports/ Construction_Trade_Convergence.pdf is a PDF by Arthur D. Little that includes useful business model information for the construction industry.

(6) *Global Food Industry* **ERS (Economic Research Service) of the USDA (U.S., Dept. of Agriculture)**
http://www.ers.usda.gov/topics/international-

markets-trade/global-food- markets/global-food-industry.aspx **"The structure of the global food industry is continually changing and evolving as food suppliers, manufacturers, and retailers adjust to meet the needs of consumers, who are increasingly demanding a wider variety of higher quality products...."**

(7) **"Regional Environment and Agriculture Programming Model (REAP)"** is the mathematical agricultural model of the U.S. Department of Agriculture's Economic Research Service, which began in 1985 as the USMP (U.S. Mathematical Programming Regional Agricultural Sector Model). *http://www.ers.usda.gov/media/201058/ tb1916fm_1_.pdf* The model *"...represents the interactions among product prices, choice of production practices, and demand for crop and livestock products when analyzing the potential effects of policies designed to address environmental issues associated with agriculture."* *"The effects of environmental and energy policies were so widespread and the interaction among the various commodities so complex that it was impossible for analysts, using the available analytical tools and research results to project the ultimate effect of specified policies on agricultural producers or even to determine whether the policies would achieve their desired goals."*

(8) "**An Analysis of the Operational Costs of Trucking: A 2014 Update,**" *http://www.atri-*

*online.org/wp-content/uploads/2014/09/ATRI-
Operational-Costs-of-Trucking-2014-FINAL.pdf*
**This is an American Transportation Research
Institute report, including a research survey.**

(9) *"A Transportation Modeling Primer"*

https://www4.uwm.edu/cuts/utp/models.pdf
*"Urban transportation planning can appear to be a
complex and bewildering process when first
encountered. This primer is intended to explain
how the process works, the assumptions
made and the steps that are used in urban
transportation planning...."   "(This document has
been incorporated into a book "Inside the
Blackbox, Making Transportation Models Work for
Livable Communities" It is available from the
Citizens for a Better Environment at 414-271-7280
or the Environmental Defense Fund
(publication 99215S)_at 202-387-3500 - public
information office)"*

(10) *"Aviation Insights Review (AIR): The Future of
Airline Business Models – Which Will Win? "
http://www.lek.com/sites/default/files/
LEK_1634_AirlineBusinessModels_Web_1.pdf*
by L.E.K. Consulting. *"L.E.K. Consulting is a global
management consulting firm that uses deep
industry expertise and analytical rigor to help
clients solve their most critical business
problems. ..."*

(11) *"2015 Media & Entertainment Industry Outlook"*

http://www2.deloitte.com/us/en/pages/technology-media-and-telecommunications/articles/2015-media-and-entertainment-outlook.html
"Media companies need to be ready for the new economic models coming their way as demand for content anywhere and anytime accelerates, according to Gerald Belson, vice chairman and U.S. Media & Entertainment leader at Deloitte Consulting, LLP."

(12) *The Trouble With Travel Distribution*
http://www.mckinsey.com/industries/travel-transport-and-logistics/our-insights/the-trouble-with-travel-distribution
"It's among the biggest e-commerce markets, and maybe its most turbulent. To compete, players must define their place in travel's next wave. ..."

(13) *A Look At The Retail Model Of The Future*
http://www.forbes.com/sites/barbarathau/2015/02/10/a-look-at-the-retail-model-of-the-future/#6f9128c117e8
"Changing consumer shopping tastes and expectations are quietly transforming the retail industry. ..."

(14) *Global banking outlook 2015: transforming banking for the next generation*
http://www.ey.com/Publication/vwLUAssets/ey-global-banking-outlook-2015-new-business-models/$FILE/EY-global-banking-outlook-2015-new-business-models.pdf

This is an Ernst &Young PDF on their view of global banking. *"Existing pressures from stakeholders, combined with the megatrends that are reshaping the world, will transform banks and their business models over the next decade. ..."*

(15) Investing in the future :How megatrends are reshaping the future of the investment management industry
https://www.kpmg.com/dutchcaribbean/en/ Documents/Publications/Investing-In-The- Future-report-fs.pdf This is a KPMG PDF on their view of the future of investment business models.

(16) *Winning Operating Models for Global Insurance Companies*
http://www.bain.com/publications/articles/winning- operating-models-for-global-insurance- companies.aspx This is an article on Bain& Co.'s view on insurance business models.

(17) *Defining a Resilient Business Model for Water Utilities*
http://www.waterrf.org/publicreportlibrary/4366.pdf This is a Water Research Foundation publication on water utility business models.

(18) *The State of the Education Industry in 2015*
http://www.edudemic.com/whoa-education-is-a-7- trillion-dollar-industry/ This is a brief summary of the education industry, with some business model information.

(19) *6 Business Models That Are Transforming Health Systems Around The World* *http://www.forbes.com/sites/ashoka/2013/06/07/6-business-models-that-are-transforming-health-systems-around-the-world/#7353ac797e75* *"The new vision for health care isn't just about access, quality and affordability. It's also about social and financial inclusion. ..."*

(20) *New Business Models and Strategies in Shipping* *http://ebooks.narotama.ac.id/files/The %20Blackwell%20Companion%20to%20Maritime %20Economics%20(Blackwell %20Companions %20to%20Contemporary%20Economics)/Chapter %2013%20%20New %20Business%20Models %20and%20Strategies%20in%20Shipping.pdf* **This is a short e-book PDF on shipping industry business models.**

The above references and web links should help the reader understand the process of tailoring a forecast to the business model of the particular company or entity. First, to understand the industry, then the company, then the brand, and or course then operational elements that need to be modeled.

3.6 MODEL DEVELOPMENT AND CALIBRATION

The above examples have shown that a causal

model can be constructed for virtually any product or service, for any channel mix, for a variety of advertising and promotion programs that are aimed at generating awareness and contacts, and for any distribution chain situation and merchandising program. But it is up to the market forecasting organization to fully coordinate the model development process and buy-in from many supporting organizations.

As part of the model development process, it is mandatory to calibrate and certify the model. To begin calibration, one merely needs to work backwards as follows. First, consider the following coarse relationship:

Forecast Base x (Aggregated Operational Factors and Pricing) x Purchase Intent = Revenue

Where: Aggregated Operational Factors and Functions = Awareness, Promotion, Supply, Merchandising, Pricing Plan and Price Level, plus Buyer Proclivity

For your model, you will have established the Forecast Base from the Targeting and Segmentation Plan, plus your demographic analysis and data mining.

From your Market Research (Secondary Research or New Primary Research), you will have obtained Purchase Intent at different pricing levels for different pricing plans

So: Aggregated Operational Factors = Revenue/ (Forecast Base x Purchase Intent)

You will then need to break down the "Aggregated Operational Factors" number into awareness, promotion, supply, merchandising, and other relevant operational factors.

From your market research, you should have included a question on general industry-level offer awareness, and also an unaided question on specific awareness for your brand. Also, from your Annual Report, you should be able to obtain a dollar figure for total advertising and promotion. You might even be able to get some sort of *"advertising effectiveness"* factors from your advertising department or from your advertising agency, but be aware that the subject of effectiveness for advertising and promotion is a touchy area, and for some brands and offers, there will be a long awareness retention and brand loyalty period, so you might end up estimating declining retention and brand loyalty curves.

Regarding supply chain and merchandising factors, you will be able to find out how many stores a packaged goods product is being stocked and displayed in, or how many distributors carry your brand, but remember that with today's online e-commerce included in the mix of distribution channels, just about 100% of your target segments should be able to order your product or service, if the offer is properly included at operationally effective websites, and buyers have web access.

So, keep accumulating factors from internal sources and from secondary research, and soon you will be able to isolate ranges of estimates for all of the factors in your forecasting model. Then you need to ask yourself: *"Are these estimates reasonable and defensible?"* When your answer is *"Yes"* then you will have completed a first round of model calibration.

Eventually, if an offer goes forward, you will have actual sales results, but many of the other factors, like the real advertising and promotion, and supply chain and merchandising, will remain unknowns for a while until real measurement and tracking data are available.

3.7 MODELING PITFALLS

Things can go wrong with modeling and forecasting. One of the most common pitfalls is to not keep track of assumptions that are being made, either by a market research or forecasting organization, or by administrative and operational groups who are part of the overall Team. Sometimes assumptions are made implicitly without even knowing that something has been assumed. Examples are awareness levels generated via advertising and promotion and merchandising, or supply chain assumptions that the inventory and supply will always be able to keep up with demand. The forecaster should make the Team aware that when you advertise a brand but don't have sufficient merchandising and supply, you often are merely driving up the sales of competitors.

Sometimes forecasters are very busy in a company and move from project to project, such that nobody is keeping track of changes that have occurred since the original forecast was produced. Often departments will stick with a prior forecast as if it is a "teflon projection" which is impervious to operational and industry changes. This failure to appreciate sensitivity to all of the factors in a model is a disastrous pitfall, and can result in profitability declines and market share losses.

At times, forecasters might operate in an isolated mode within a company, and fail to get buy-in from all stakeholders affected. If support elements in a project Team fail to respond to sign-off requests, the issue must be escalated so that a higher level of management is aware of the situation and the severe implications of making incorrect assumptions in the forecasting and modeling for a project.

Over-analysis and analysis-paralysis can be ingrown diseases within some forecasting and market research organizations. It has been said that *"Done is better that perfection,"* meaning that at some point a modeling and forecasting effort needs to freeze and go with the results up to that point. This of course all depends on what is appropriate for the prioritization and strategic importance of a project.

3.8 FORECAST SIMULATION

One great advantage of the modeling approach to forecasting is the ability to generate mechanized simulations quickly and in response to questions and issues that arise. Once a model is formulated it will force buy-in suggestions and the finalization of assumptions.

But make sure that you do not start this simulation phase until the model is on firm ground and will not result in any of the support organizations failing to come together for a consensus. The best way to do this is to keep your data sources closely held so that nobody goes around you to a research supplier or a data mining source. You want to avoid this type of spurious challenge at all cost.

The first simulations you will want to generate are *"best and worst case scenarios."* There will be a big judgment factor in doing best and worst case scenarios, but in general you don't want to get carried away with scenario cases that are unrealistically optimistic or too pessimistic.

If the project is an "investment spending" initiative, there still will be limits on initial losses that will be tolerated, with the assumption that market share will be obtained by incurring losses. You can make this more realistic by creating a simulation scenario in which it is assumed that at some point competitors will see any new innovation on the market and then copy it in some fashion, even with a cheap *"knock off offering"* of their own.

For simulation using your forecast model, make sure that you keep track of *"what if questions"* in an orderly manner and don't let control of the forecasting process become unglued. Some on your Team might come up with unreasonable what-ifs with which you do not want to be associated.

3.9 KEEPING ANY MODEL UP TO DATE

It goes without saying that an obsolete model and an old forecast is not only worthless but also dangerous if misused. For security, you should be keeping a "need-to-know" list of who was originally given a copy of any model or forecast, either paper or electronically, but of course you cannot control who else they might distribute such to, in violation of strict security rules and sanctions. When any model and forecast are originally distributed and publicized internally, there should always be a strong caveat issued about not only security and confidentiality and competitive concerns, but a strong notice that any future versions of the forecast will completely replace what is being distributed originally.

3.10 MODELING STRATEGIC DECISIONS

"Wherever you see a successful business, someone once made a courageous decision." "Doing the right thing is more important than doing the  *thing right" "There is nothing quite so useless as doing with great efficiency something that should not be done at all."*

- Peter Drucker, 1909-2005

What Is Strategic - Reviewed

As noted in Section 1.2, a strategic decision usually will change the *mission statement* and the

114

business model of an entity. Now we will go beyond that in the further discussion which follows.

It sounds simple, but the way to start modeling a strategic decision is to create two models, namely both *before* and *after* the decision is actually implemented, and then to analyze the difference. And this is usually done for a number of possible alternative opportunities and scenarios. The models generally will be focused on both the market and the financial outcomes for these alternatives. But the model for any strategic decision must also identify what is needed both operationally, administratively, and legally, for the strategic scenario to be actually implemented.

Market Potential For Strategic Decision-Making

Often, rather than generating detailed demand forecasts for strategic scenarios, it is best to first determine the *gross market potential* associated with the proposed strategic decision. For an innovation, it is necessary to first ask if the innovation can be converted to a real market opportunity. Will it be worthwhile to incur the expenses required? Is the potential market for the innovation so large that even a very conservative market share will pay for the development, assuming expenses are under control ? Is an innovation already in the public domain? If so, competitors might already have developed early internal prototypes. Remember also, that just because competitors might display a prototype at a trade show, this does not mean that they are going ahead with final development, production and marketing. They might

115

even want to license the innovation off to someone else.

So alternative scenarios and associated market potential are the first step. Even if a merger-acquisition seems like a good idea at the time, and passes financial criteria, ultimately it will be the *market demand* that will determine success. Trying to justify a strategic decision solely because of "perceived efficiency gains" is usually a path to failure, since the market will ultimately be the deciding factor, not hoped-for operational efficiencies and tricks. Also, gaining market share via an acquisition or predatory decision also is not a prescription for success. Some acquisitions are purely to put a competitor out of business, and lay off most of their staff, but this itself can have negative consequences. Getting a bigger share of a market that is going to decline and be changed because of new competitive business models or new innovations is also a wrong decision. It is better to have a smaller market share in growing and profitable markets than a large share in a market which is soon to decline, and for which fixed costs cannot move fast enough to prevent declining profitability or big losses.

Sometimes secondary research can be used to estimate market potential, but be careful if such research is a multiclient study in the public domain, since this means that the idea is already out there and you might not be able to catch up with competitors who have already started their own projects. But *proprietary* research and focus groups, if done securely, can be used to uncover market potential that others have yet to know about. Or, if your company has demonstrated that they are more adept

116

at converting innovations into business opportunities, then it is OK to go ahead and try to outpace competitors.

A company or any business or governmental entity "needs to know themselves" as a prerequisite to making an important strategic decision.

Mission Statements And Business Models

Almost any strategic decision will disturb or modify the mission statement, and also the business model of an entity, so it is imperative to analyze and document exactly how both the mission statement and business model will change, because of the strategic decision. This must be done in a disciplined manner, with supporting analysis, and should not be treated lightly.

You must honestly ask "are we getting into uncharted waters ?" and "are we biting off more that we can chew ?" Just because a smaller company acquires a larger company does not mean that they are over their head, but all of the issues must be analyzed and forecasted accordingly. Conversely, just because a large company wants to acquire a smaller entity, and "see if we can make it work" does not mean that it will be a good decision, and that there might be better alternatives.

When industries are changing rapidly and companies wait too late to adapt, sometimes they lose out on an opportunity and begin to decline. And some companies have learned from experience that it is not wise to always operate on the "leading-bleeding edge" and best to be a cautious market follower who can swoop in rapidly if an opportunity is real and others have been unable to capitalize on the opportunity because they do not know how to execute properly.

To hang on in a declining market until events take control can be a disaster. Kodak was in denial about digital photography replacing chemical and silver-halide photography, and eventually went out of business. Nokia and RIM (Blackberry) did not move fast enough into the smartphone mobile device market and lost big to Apple and Samsung and others. Apple was a computer company and was adept at restating their mission statement and business model to become a major mobile device company, as well as a major music distribution company.

Decision Support Systems (DSS)

There are many software templates, information systems, and databases which purport to aid and support the decision process, and these have become known as DSS (Decision Support Systems). A overview of DSS can be found in *References 12 and 13*.

Of course, just about everything useful that you might identify can support a decision, but the idea of a DSS is a software platform that aids decision-making when the problem is particularly unstructured and it does this through the use of user-friendly interfaces and enhanced GUI (graphic user interface) displays and presentation formats. Therefore, in many cases DSS can be useful in matters involving strategic decisions.

Closely related to DSS are *"executive dashboard"* systems (*Reference 14*) and *"MIS (Management Information Systems)."* Many companies utilize these in both formal and informal applications to organize information and support decision-making.

The primary caveat regarding DSS, Dashboard, and MIS is that one must never let the software itself limit the scope or nature of a decision. A strategic decision especially requires that any support system or information be customized and adapted to the here-and-now, to the problem under consideration, and to the culture and environment of the entity.

3.11 CONFIDENTIALITY, SECURITY, TIMING, AND ETHICS

Throughout this entire book, the matter of "need-to-know," for your documents and files has been mentioned. But it is worth reemphasizing here the importance of this.

- There are hackers around the world, some being sponsored by their governments, and some freelance hackers who try to sell what they find to the highest bidder, be it a governmental, corporate, or terrorist entity.

- Competitors are always trying to find out what others are doing or planning, but will

119

often do this through third parties to keep under the radar.

- There is always a balance between transparency for public relations, investor relations, trade show presence, and sales aggressiveness, versus the need to keep competitors and hackers in the dark. Manage this balance carefully.

Regarding secondary research and data mining, be skeptical and try to confirm information sources. There is a lot of bad data, obsolete data, and irrelevant data online. You do not want to use any of this bad data.

Also, the matter of ethics is important in the entire integrated process of decision support, forecasting, modeling, and business cases. Internally, any forecasting entity needs to build a solid reputation for producing forecasts that will positively aid decisions, either administrative, operational, or strategic in nature. One bad instance can spread irreparable damage, so always have in place a strong *quality assurance process* for research, modeling, forecasting, and business cases. And externally, research suppliers and consultants must equally maintain the highest ethics and quality control stature to protect their brand.

3.12 MODELING & FORECASTING SOFTWARE

Little is done manually in a well-managed and up

-to-date research, forecasting, or business case organization. Either they will have developed their own software platforms or they will have licensed the best that they can find for each particular project. *Appendix C* includes a listing of some of the market research, forecasting, and business case software that is available. This book does not endorse or recommend any of these packages or platforms, but these are listed to aid the reader. The reader is advised to access the websites of these and obtain a test copy for their own evaluation and applicability to the particular project.

*****

PART FOUR

BUSINESS CASES AND PLANNING

"If you fail to plan, you are planning to fail,"
Benjamin Franklin *(probably in Poor Richard's
Almanack, 1733-1758)*

4.1 - ORCHESTRATING THE ENTIRE PROCESS

The core of a successful *Business Plan* for any organization is the *orchestration* of a wide range of issues, organizational elements, and information to make sure that the assumptions and methodologies are all consistent. If market research, either secondary or primary, plus data mining, does not support assumptions and forecasts, then the business plan will fall apart and there will be numerous challenges for a decision to proceed, or even worse, the organization will proceed without the needed support and eventually the organization will face failure.

This is true whether the forecast is being used in a business case or a business plan, or as a key element in a strategic decision, or to support an administrative or operational change. This might sound easy, but it requires a high degree of skill, knowledge, and experience.

In today's rich computing environment, mechanization of the entire process of primary and secondary market research, data mining, forecasting and business case development is possible and highly desirable. This type of integration and full mechanization will make possible a fully linked flow-through of changes in assumptions and new data, as well as rapid sensitivity analysis.

This Part Four outlines the steps that must be followed in order to correctly manage the interrelated market research, forecasting, and business case process.

Typically many cross-organizational resources are required to develop a valid forecast. It is the job of the forecasting entity, either with an organization or on outside contract, to make sure that these resources are well managed and that there is open communication throughout the program. It is usually necessary for the management of a forecasting entity, either in-house or on contract, to conduct a number of forecasting projects at the same time, managing skills and allocating resources optimally. Part of this management is to make sure that different fiefdoms do not confuse senior management and stakeholders with differing views and results.

Forecasts Are Key In A Business Case Or Plan

A business case is itself a *forecast:"If we do _____ then the following result will occur."* It is a proposal for a decision, and the business plan provides a complete operational, administrative and financial statement of what

123

is needed to implement the decision.

The difference between a Business Plan and a Business Case is that a Business Plan is company-wide and includes all of the operational, administrative, execution, and scheduling details needed to implement the recommendation, whereas a Business Case is a proposal for a decision, stating the benefits that will accrue from that decision. In a Business Case, there are forecasts of revenues and margins over time, and in a Business Plan, there are forecasts of not only revenues and margins, but also forecasts of expenses over the planning period, including for such things as facilities and equipment, human resources and personnel, advertising and promotion, inventory and distribution, billing and accounting, and legal considerations.

It is very useful for an entity to maintain a *business case portfolio*, namely an organized and updated collection of business cases for initiatives which could be executed at the proper time, and via the in-place decision process of that entity. However, most organizations merely generate a business case when there is a proposal to be considered here-and-now, and this can result in a last-minute schedule pressure.

Sometimes a Business Case will begin by stating, for example, *"If we invest $100M dollars in the latest innovation developed by our R&D organization, then after the introduction of the new product, we will earn an additional $30M over a five year period. If we proceed, we will negate our competitors. If we don't do this, our* *competitors are planning to introduce a similar product and we will miss an opportunity to be the leader for this new area."*

The first Part of this book emphasized the relationship between *decisions* and *forecasts*, namely that any decision has a closely related forecast or at a minimum an implied prediction of the outcome of the decision. But in most cases, especially in the case of *strategic decisions*, more than a forecast is needed. The strategic forecast is based on many assumptions and usually includes proposed business model changes, which must be fully documented and confirmed, and all of this, including alternatives and consequences, should be formulated as a *business plan*.

Many think of a business case or a business plan as merely a financial proposal for a course of action. This is not a complete view. It is true that most strategic business plans involve a proposal for investment in a new course of action, like a merger-acquisition, an expansion, a diversification, or a joint venture. Conversely, there may be a financial proposal for a major force reduction, getting out of a business area, substantially modifying the business model, major refinancing, a spin-off, selling off the company, or a liquidation. But the financial numbers, like margins or EBITA (earnings before interest, taxes, and amortization) are merely one output of any proposal. The heart of the matter is a set of assumptions and then related forecasts that flow from a model of the actions, and finally the resulting dollar numbers. Not just revenues must be forecasted, but also expenses, resources, and operational and administrative elements.

So the heart of the business case or plan is modeling the proposal(s) in all aspects, then simulation of alternatives which include marketing, administrative, and operational assumptions. If any of the assumptions change, then the elements in the modeling change, and the forecasts and financial numbers change. Often best-case and a worst-case scenarios will be simulated. But a note of caution here. Sometimes financial-only organizations are in charge of a business case and they will modify financial numbers at-will without going back to important assumptions regarding marketing and operational matters. *This kind of raw and uncoordinated modification to a business case generates invalid results and can lead to incorrect and disastrous decisions.*

Forecasts with a full set of assumptions are applied in a business case to an applicable *business model*, which can vary all the way from a holding company, licensing, total subcontracting and outsourcing, to a highly vertically integrated operation. And the proposed plans can be highly focused on one recommended course of action, or can present a range of options so that a strategic decision can be made on the business model and other strategic priorities.

This book is not focused on the business case or business plan itself - there are many works covering that subject. Rather, the focus is on the forecasting process as it concerns decisions and the related business models and related business cases that go with these business models.

4.2 MISSION STATEMENTS AND BUSINESS MODELS

It is a very strategic decision for an entity to decide on the correct business model. For example, they might have an R&D organization which constantly develops and patents new innovations. These innovations might merely be an improvement to a current offering, or might be something totally unique which could even start a new industry. What to do with this kind of innovation? Form a new division to go further? License it off because it is not related to the current business model, or would it take too much financing and resources to go further? Look to form a joint venture with others who could add synergy and lead to a successful new market offering? And of course, is the idea worth anything in the marketplace? These are strategic decisions, which must be based on some kind of forecast for the innovation as an offering in the real world. If such a forecast cannot be attempted at this time, then perhaps the innovative development needs to to go further, including prototypes and market tests, and will these next steps be worth the money and resources? Perhaps the company has a disciplined *phased development process* and that the idea is not ready for the next phase. *Converting innovations to business opportunities* is an important function that should be built into any organization which develops new ideas.

Can technical people alone be trusted to produce sufficient early forecasts for strategic decision making? Usually not. Usually there needs to be a team effort of people who know about *converting innovations to business opportunities,* and they will be an important factor in deciding on the appropriate business model. Somebody has to stick their neck out and produce numbers that can help determine the value of an innovation.

Some entities like to keep things simple, and not "get their hands dirty" with extended development, and like to operate merely as an R&D company, that licenses off innovations and keeps a percentage of the deals in case something really takes off. Or a holding company that looks around for things to license, which they can then pass along to others who can turn the innovation into a real business opportunity. Other entities like to remain very much involved in development of an offering, in order to maintain strict security and confidentiality and control, but leave open the option of future licensing and possible joint ventures. And other entities like to control everything to make sure that it all is done "right." Apple is a company harboring this kind of control, but as we know, they still offshore most of their manufacturing to Foxconn and Inventec in China. *(This is totally separate from any Apple financial offshoring.)*

Some Types of Business Models

Business models can vary from the simple to the highly complex and convoluted, which challenge the governing regulatory and legal limitations. For purely tax purposes, the IRS lists the following five business model categories:

- Sole Proprietorships *(one owner, but could have other employees)*

- Partnerships *(multiple owners who have their own agreement and file separate taxes)*

- Corporations *(stock entities, both non-profit and for-profit, with no individual liabilities)*

- S Corporations *(corporations with individual shareholder taxes and liabilities)*

- LLCs (Limited Liability Companies) *(liabilities separated and state-level regulations apply)*

Beyond the above IRS categories, here are some of the many types of possible business models.

- Vertically Integrated Model *(attempt to own the supply chain and manufacturing from raw materials to the final finished goods, and even the supply chain, keeping all supporting functions in-house)*

- Horizontally Integrated Model *(provides a mix of similar products or services across a wide spectrum of industry segments; example is ADP - Automatic Data Processing - which provides payroll and accounting outsourcing services for many entities in many segments)*

- Outsourcing Model *(keep in-house functions to a minimum, and outsource to others as much as possible, but control the brands and intellectual property, maintaining non-compete and exclusivity agreements as needed)*

- **Offshoring Model** *(outsourcing but sending almost all functions to a lower-cost country, possibly with less control of intellectual property and less non-compete enforcement)*

- **Subcontracting Model** *(similar to outsourcing model, but usually with more control over quality and intellectual property)*

- **Direct Retail Model** *(owner-operator of retail stores or online websites which sell products or services directly to end-users, and for online sales will utilize various final distribution and fulfillment services; sometimes merely a drop-ship entity that passes along sales orders)*

- **Wholesaler Model** *(providing a go-between that holds inventory from manufacturers and distributes this inventory to either direct retailers or other distributors in the supply chain; can either own the inventory or merely hold it for a fee or on a consignment basis)*

- **Catalog Direct Model** *(same as a Direct Retailer, but with awareness and advertising primarily via paper catalogs, and telephone or online ordering)*

- **Holding Company Model** *(the entity is a non-*

operating business, but owns a significant control in one or more other entities, which themselves could be operational or also secondary holding companies, but sometimes with control of intellectual property and exclusivity and non-compete rights)

- Shell Company Model *(a paper-only variation of a holding company, often to separate liabilities, or to avoid taxes in an actual operating jurisdiction, or even for illegally misrepresenting a brand or for illegally laundering funds)*

- Partnership Model *(a group of individuals or entities which are bound by their own private legal agreement, for the purpose of providing services or a particular secondary business function)*

- Joint Venture Model *(a grouping of two or more individuals or entities, each of whom usually have additional interests, for the purpose of developing a particular market area or service, on a permanent or temporary basis)*

- Contract Manufacturing Model *(an operating entity that provides manufacturing services for others, and usually is bound by exclusivity and non-compete agreements to not do contract manufacturing for competitive products)*

- Licensing Model *(ownership or temporary rights of intellectual property like patents, brands and*

131

trademarks, but no operational functions; degree of control and quality assurance of the final offering can vary)

- **Brand and Trademark-Only Model** *(version of a licensing model but with no licensing of intellectual property and patents, and merely collecting fees for brand and trademark usage, that is, putting a brand identification on an offering)*

- **Agent and Broker Models** *(providing a go-between to represent sellers and buyers in a transaction, usually on a temporary basis, but could also be subject to a more extended agreement; example: real estate brokers and stock transaction brokers)*

- **Consulting Model** *(providing services through an agreement, usually subject to non-compete but usually not exclusive, for the purpose of advising an entity on a course of action)*

- **Advertising Models** *(entities which often do not control any products or services themselves, but merely make money off advertising for the offerings of others, such as Google; radio and broadcast TV offer free programs and make their money via advertising; however most of TV is now via cable subscription plus pay-per-view)*

- **Franchise Model** *(growing a business geographically via repeat of the original business model through contracted individuals and entities*

*who pay an initial amount to own a franchise
territory and must adhere to a tight agreement on
the offering and pay revenue royalties to the
franchising organization; the franchisees almost
always must purchase exclusively through the
franchising organization on their stated terms and
conditions; example: fast food franchises, oil-
change franchises, hotel-motel chains, sports
franchises like the NFL)*

- **Affiliate Model** *(usually a loose form of a franchise,
  acting merely as a sales agent for a particular
  offering, and usually not granting territorial
  exclusivity, but merely a drop-ship go-between with
  no inventory, but with prospecting and advertising
  and sales rights)*

- **Auction Model** *(providing a go-between for a
  transaction between sellers and buyers, with the
  final offering price determined by the buyers, and
  sometimes an initial price determined by the
  sellers, and hopefully with no liability on the part of
  the auction entity; example: E-Bay)*

- **Customer Lock-In Model** *(an up-front attractive
  offering, usually below actual cost and sometimes
  totally free, which then locks in the buyer for a
  contract period or simply because of the
  exclusivity of some needed follow-on services or
  product elements; examples: cellphone devices
  with cell service contracts; also razors and blades
  example)*

- **Subscription Model** *(end-users pay an ongoing fee for an ongoing service or a periodic delivery of a product or service, as opposed to a one-time payment, and usually get a discount for subscribing; sometimes pre-paid subscription is also offered; examples are pay-TV, magazines, vitamins)*

- **Knock-Off Model** *(waiting for another entity to offer a particular service or product, and then if it is successful, offering a similar product or service, which gets around any branding or intellectual property rights, and is often offered at a lower price and lesser quality, and often only for a limited period, with a very limited warranty it at all)*

- **Freemium Model** *(gives a free offering to start, but tries to get customers to upgrade and pay a premium for additional features or services)*

- **Bricks & Clicks Model** *(order online but pick up the item at a physical store, hopefully to drive traffic that will buy additional items; the reverse of this is showrooming, wherein customers look at a product in a physical store, including demos and assistance, but then go home and make the purchase online or buy something else online at a better price)*

- **Platform Model** *(primarily for software offerings, an API - application programming interface, is defined* *and then a SDK - software development kit, is made available so that 3rd parties can develop useful offerings, called "apps" to end-users, either free or for a charge. This relieves the device manufacturer and platform originator from spending time and resources on specialized software routines that add value. In the mobile phone environment, companies like Apple and Samsung database many thousands of available third-party apps.)*

- **MLM or Party Plan Model** *(multilevel marketing and party plan marketing utilize trained and authorized agents who generate leads and sales through friends, family, and associates, and often have group presentations in their homes; if multiple levels of marketing are established after the business begins to grow, then the initial authorized agent will use group presentations to train the lower level of agents, and then eventually they might also establish lower level agents themselves)*

- **Cloud-Based Services Model** *(for software, users do not install individually licensed copies of a software offering on their premises-based machines, but merely access shared servers via networking or the Internet; this also includes SaaS, software-as-a-service offerings)*

Note that many business entities will engage in several variations of the above business models at the same time, for different offerings, so as to simultaneously maintain a portfolio mix of offerings and business models.

This mix is managed carefully so as to not damage any brand equity and to maximize the gain on any intellectual property that they control.

A business or governmental entity should be able to tailor the business model for any new idea or changes to the innovation itself, but at the same time have a *core business model* which fits their fundamental *mission statement*. To further this understanding, here are some examples of *business models* for both business and governmental entities.

- DARPA (Defense Advanced Research Projects Administration), founded in 1958, is an entity within the U.S. Defense Department that maintains a staff to support their mission to generate, monitor, and develop ideas which have value to the overall U.S. economy and in particular will further the U.S. national defense. In 1969 DARPA sponsored a network called ARPANET between the University of California and Stanford Research Institute, and it went operational, and this was the beginning of what has today become the Internet. Eventually, management of the Internet moved to the NSF (National Science Foundation), and today it is a cooperative international public information network, overseen technically mostly by the IETF (Internet Engineering Task Force). So the DARPA business model is to develop and nurture technical ideas which will enhance the defense of the U.S., but it does not manufacture nor license anything. It accomplishes its mission through grants, funding of initiatives, and demonstration projects

- PTTs *(Post, Telephone and Telegraph entities, originally wholly owned and operated by governments worldwide, with their revenues part of the general government revenues; then many of these spunoff significant shares of their telecommunications operations and raised billions of dollars; many countries still operate these PTT structures as part of their governments)*

- Deutche Telekom AG *(Originally Deutche Bundepost after WW2, is the German PTT and telecommunications company, which is 32% government-owned, 15% directly and 17% through the government bank; DT owns and operates many telecommunications entities, including the U.S. T-Mobile wireless service provider.)*

- Apple, Inc. was started in 1976 and incorporated as Apple Computers in 1977. But Apple changed its name to Apple, Inc. in 2007 to reflect is change in business model from a PC manufacturer to a consumer electronics and services company. Apple is a hardware supplier *(iPad, iPhone, iPod, and MAC PC products)*, a software supplier *(OS-X, iOS, Safari, iTunes media player, iLife and iWork suites)*, services supplier *(iTunes online store, iOS App online store, MAC App online store, and iCloud online)*, and lastly a direct retailer, with over 500 *Apple Stores* worldwide. *Apple is said to have an inverted razor/blades business model for its iPod at a high price and music/videos offered through iTunes at a low price)*

- **Comcast Holdings owns NBCUniversal** *(an international media producer of films and TV programs),* **is a cable TV and airwave TV operator** *(NBC, Telemundo, E!, Golf Channel, NBCSN),* **a film producer** *(Universal Pictures),* **an entertainment parks operator** *(Universal Theme Parks),* **and holds other multimedia, cable-TV and telecommunications interests. Therefore, Comcast is a multinational multimedia conglomerate.**

- **Eastman Kodak Company** *(originally a highly vertically integrated manufacturer which dominated the silver-halide and chemical-based film industry. Kodak misjudged and resisted the transition to digital photography based on charged-coupled electronic device arrays which now provide megapixel photographic resolution, dominated by electronic products like the smartphone; Kodak underwent bankruptcy proceedings, and the only surviving entity is UK-based Kodak Alaris, owned by the UK-based Kodak Pension Plan, and focusing solely on personalized imaging and document imaging.)*

- **Western Electric** *(originally a captive manufacturing division of the AT&T Bell System, was a prime example of a vertically integrated manufacturer; owned a coal mine for high grade anthracite which was ground up and processed to*

138

make telephone microphones, made its own screws, transformers, metal parts, and product plastic housings; bought from outside only stainless steel rolls, plastic pellets, and other fundamental raw materials; was spun off as Lucent Technologies and then merged with Alcatel to form Lucent-Alcatel, a supplier of global telecommunications equipment)

- Uber Technologies, Inc. *(an online transportation network, Uber offers a smartphone app which links prospective riders to registered Uber drivers to set up the submitted trip; the Uber Co. charges a commission on the rides set up through its platform)*

- Tesla Motors, Inc. *(an electric car company whereby Tesla buyers pay up front in the price of the car for ten years worth of electric energy, to be derived via the Tesla Supercharger network)*

4.3 BUSINESS CASE ELEMENTS

The purpose of a business case is to propose and support a decision on a particular matter. A business case must cover a number of areas in order to do this, and the emphasis among these areas depends on the stakeholders and final decision-makers. Business cases take many different styles, from a few pages of financial numbers to a large multi-volume document that is complemented by an elaborate multi-media presentation.

139

The following are a few of the fundamental elements which should be included in any business case.

(1) A business case report, whether on paper or electronically or via a presentation, should start with an *Executive Summary* that states the *Recommendation* and includes financial summaries and a summary of the financial and market benefits.

(2) Secondly, a business case should then state the *Opportunity*, be it a strategic decision like an acquisition or merger or an operational decision like investing in a new innovation or taking advantage of a market situation. This is where new primary market research should be summarized, or at least secondary research and data mining findings, in support of the stated Opportunity, and a total market analysis including market potential and forecasted revenues.

(3) Third, a *Competitive Analysis* should be summarized, including any comparable offerings that currently exist or are about to be offered. Market share should be stated, both for doing nothing and for after implementation of the business case recommendation.

(4) All *Expenses* and costs should be stated next, including both direct and indirect costs, in such categories as human resources and organizational requirements, new hiring, new facilities needed, new operational and distribution expenses, and new advertising and promotional expenses, as required to

implement the Recommendation.

(5) In each of the above business case Sections, *Assumptions* should be explicitly stated as part of that Section.

(6) Lastly, *Alternatives* to the primary Recommendation should be stated, and a *Sensitivity Analysis* should be summarized for the important parameters in the Recommendation. The null-alternative should always be included here. Most basically, a business case proposes that *"If you do this, the positive result will be the following."* So even at the most basic level, a business case is a forecast.

In addition to the above generic list of the elements of a business case, there are many references that can be consulted. For example, Reference 4 *(listed in the Reference and Sources Section at the back of this book)* lists five elements:

(1) A Scenario Analysis
(2) A Definition of Cause and Effect Linkage for Each
        Proposed Benefit
(3) The Key Performance Indicator for Each Projected
        Benefit,
(4) The Risk of Doing Nothing
(5) Alignment With Strategic Goals.

As a second example, Reference 6, lists the following twelve items to be included in a business case:

1. A brief, compelling, service-oriented problem statement
2. A mission statement or vision of the future that addresses the problem
3. A description of the specific objectives to be achieved
4. A description and rationale for your preferred approach
5. A statement of the benefits that address the concerns of all relevant stakeholders
6. Measures for gauging improved performance or progress toward each objective
7. A statement of the likely risks of your initiative and how they will addressed
8. A basic plan of work with a timeline and key milestones
9. A project management plan and names and roles of key managers
10. Alternatives considered and how they would or would not work
11. Cost estimates and potential sources of funding
12. Opposing arguments and your responses to them

There are also several Plans which are separate from the Business Plan and detail the programs to make it all happen. Here are details on these related Plans.

- The *Product Plan* defines the offer and its prioritization in the overall offer mix of the organization. The Product Plan includes a statement of features, functions, and attributes, a Technical Assessment of the offer, and also a statement of the related warranty and servicing plan that supports the offer.

- The *Marketing Plan* states the target segments and why these are chosen, as well as the sales plan, the channel mix, positioning, competitive analysis, pricing levels, pricing plans, payment plans, promotion and awareness plans, advertising, co-marketing, distribution, and merchandising. The revenue and volume forecasts in the Marketing Plan reference the market research that was performed and the Modeling process used to develop the forecasts, including statement of the assumptions that were made.

- The *Operational Plan* defines the manufacturing, procurement, subcontracting, outsourcing, delivery, inventory, shipping, and quality assurance efforts.

- The *Human Resources Plan* outlines the organizational requirements, the skills, and the training needed to make the proposed program a reality.

- The *Financial Plan* includes a balance sheet and income statement for the program, spread over the projected life of the product or service, and states a number of financial indices, including ROI (return on investment), sources of funds like new borrowing or internal cash flow, financial agreements required (for investment and outsourcing), and a break-even analysis.

This all might sound like a lot to those who are not initiated in the business plan process, but it should be noted that even the most successful products or services in use today, have often started off with a "*back of the envelope business case*" based on a visionary conceptualization of a new idea, but eventually these ideas were fully developed and went through the full business case process, sometimes in repetitive cycles.

So a business case is not a "big deal." It might sound scary or even academic to some persons. But in actual fact, the term "*back of the envelope business case*" has been around for a long time to denote a quick and preliminary process of thinking through a decision in an organized manner, and leaving the process of a complete business case to be addressed at a later time.

A business plan will often define a *Phased Development Program* in which there are defined *Phase Gates* where the status of the program is audited and progress against the goals and objectives of the current phase are assessed, and a decision is made to: (1) Go ahead to the next Phase, or (2) Stay in the current Phase until certain tasks are completed, or (3) Terminate the program at this point. The idea of a Phased Development Program is to commit dollars and resources on a gradual basis, in keeping with realization of goals and objectives of the program, and to not over-commit too early in the development of an offering.

144

But remember that a business plan is first and foremost focused around a *forecast* or a range of forecasts, in order to lay out what will happen when there is a decision made and there is a related investment of dollars and resources. Even a "back of the envelope business case" must include a preliminary forecast of what will happen if the proposed decision that is being advocated in the business case is approved.

4.4 BUSINESS CASE ASSUMPTIONS

It is extremely important to keep track of and document all assumptions that are made in developing a business case. These assumptions include even the most basic facts and data that underlie the particular proposal. Sometimes analysts get so involved in number crunching that they forget they are assuming that a market for the proposed idea actually exists and will also exist in the future, and that operational and administrative factors needed to make it all happen can also be developed.

The *Executive Summary* of a business case or a business plan should always summarize the most important and fundamental assumptions that are being made. For example, if the business case is for a proposed innovation that has been developed by R&D but has not yet gone further, then a basic assumption is that this innovation can actually be successfully converted into a marketable offering, be it a product or service. Another example is the pricing plan and pricing level that was assumed in order to produce financial numbers, along

145

with the business model assumed, be it direct sales, licensing, wholesaling, franchising, and so forth. Obviously one cannot put a financial value on a proposal without both pricing and business model assumptions.

Beyond assumptions stated in the Executive Summary of a business case, each individual Section, be it the Marketing Plan, the Product Plan, the Distribution Plan or others, should contain all of the related assumptions being made in that portion of the overall plan. Nothing is too trivial or obvious regarding these supporting assumptions. For example, a Distribution Plan often will assume that distribution to a stated number of target market areas can be achieved, and that end-retail units will actually buy and inventory and merchandise the offering correctly. Another assumption in a Marketing Plan is that advertising and promotion will successfully generate a stated level of awareness, at both the end-user and the retailer levels.

4.5 ALTERNATIVES AND SIMULATIONS

The assumptions made in a business case or a business plan should all be subject to sensitivity analysis. This is one of the important reasons that a market model and an operational model should always be included in the process for development of the plan. Not all variables in the assumptions need to be analyzed for sensitivity, but prior to any final decision, it should be anticipated that numerous questions will arise, and so the capability for sensitivity analysis should be built into the process.

146

Almost always, a "best case" and a "worst case" and a "do nothing case" should be included. One should be prepared that, even at the last minute in the process, a final decision-maker might ask what will happen if competition should offer a similar product or service, perhaps one year after the go-ahead for the proposed action, and perhaps at a lower price.

When there are many unknowns in the environment, or when a proposal in a business plan involves something entirely new to the industry, it is important that a number of alternatives be analyzed and then stated in the Executive Summary. For example, the business model alternatives like licensing or a joint venture might be applicable when there are too many unknowns to commit to a go-ahead at this time and to incur a costly in-house development of a product or service.

4.6 TEAMING FOR BUSINESS CASE DEVELOPMENT

A business case and especially a complete business plan requires the orchestration of activities across organizational lines, and a *Business Case Team* must be formed and managed for development of this complete business plan. Sometimes a Product Manager will lead the business case effort, and in some organizations, either marketing or finance will take the lead. This depends on the nature of the company's business model, as well as the nature of the offer that is the focus of the business plan. Some organizations are marketing-oriented and marketing calls the shots and takes the lead for all business plans. In other cases, organizations are financially-oriented and finance is in charge of business case development. But however it is organized, business plan development remains a team effort, with many cross-organizational elements and tasks to be properly coordinated and orchestrated.

One important reason for business case teaming is buy-in on the part of all areas within an organization, especially those who must implement the decision. A business case will remain a useless pile of paper or computer files if it is not actually committed to by the entire organization. In fact, this commitment must be enthusiastic, given that implementation and adhering to schedules will usually encounter numerous issues and roadblocks. Secondly, the synergistic involvement of team members will always produce a better plan than the singular thinking of merely a few isolated individuals.

Ideally, a Business Case Team will consist of persons exclusively dedicated to the effort and getting the offering into being. This will help speed up the process and assure that no one element is holding up the overall program. However, this is the ideal and not always possible, given limited human resources in an organization.

4.7 PROJECT MANAGEMENT OF THE OVERALL PROCESS

Orchestration of a forecasting and business case

project is best done using project management tools and processes. There are many of these available online, and most of these utilize some form of a *Gantt Chart* with varying GUI interfaces. *(This type of project management tool originated as a bar chart representation by Karol Adamieski in 1896 and by Henry Gantt in the early 20th century.)* A Gantt chart starts with a listing of project tasks and deliverables that must be accomplished, and identifies a start date and an end date for each task, and also shows the interdependency of these tasks. The graphical representation of the project lists the tasks on the ordinate scale (y-axis), and the time scheduling is noted on the abscissa scale (x-axis).

Every forecasting and business case project must get off to a proper start, so the orchestration process must begin by reaffirming the *mission statement* and *business model* applicable to the project, and then stating the *goals and objectives* of the project.

The Integrated Process diagram of Figure 3, which was presented earlier in this book, is repeated on the next page for reference.

Figure 3 (repeated)

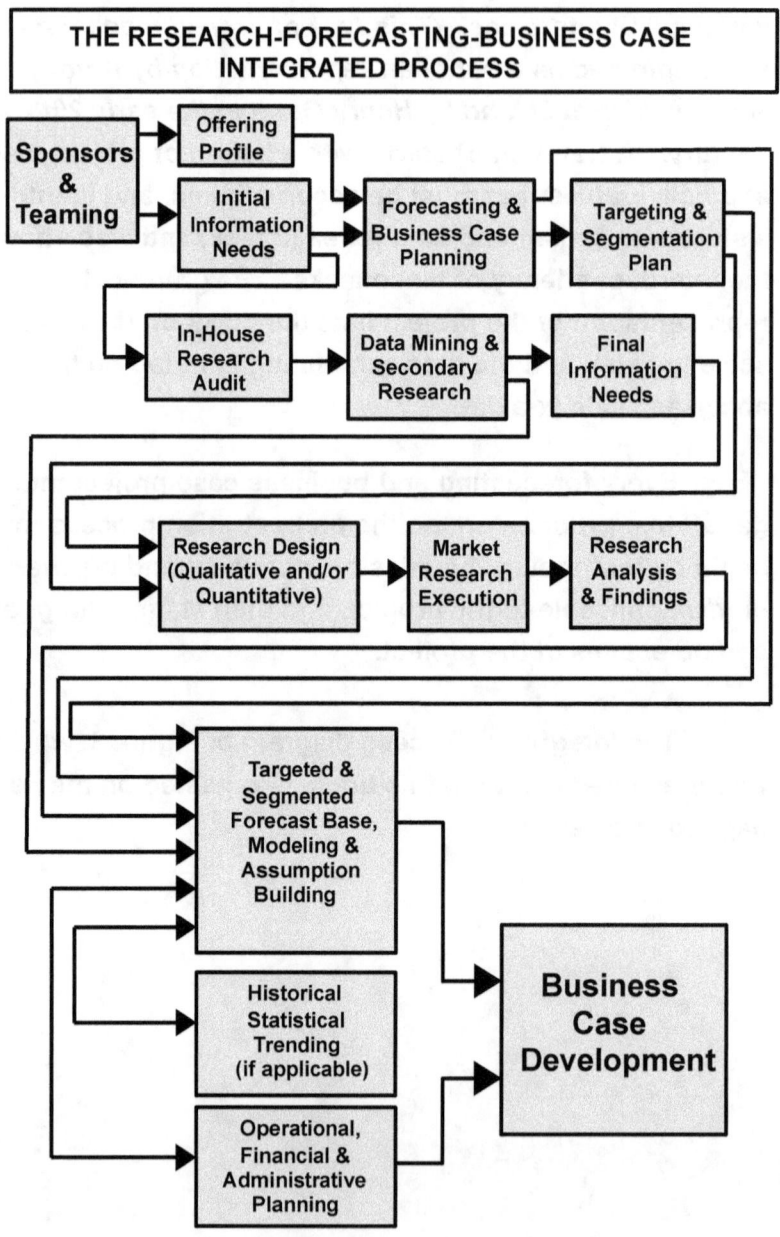

THE RESEARCH-FORECASTING-BUSINESS CASE INTEGRATED PROCESS

When developing project management and Gantt chart tools, reference should be made back to the above Integrated Process as a guide.

Finally, the following are some guidelines for controlling and managing the forecast aspects of the project.

(1) Documenting, explaining, presenting and defending forecasts

Everything done to produce a forecast must be fully documented, but with strict security and a need-to-know within the organization. This is very important for comparing and prioritizing offerings, and for later reference in the future when new projects arise.

(2) Living with the forecast

Once a forecast is finalized and there is total buy-in of all assumptions in the program, it is important that everybody in an organization falls behind the forecast and that there is no "second guessing." Actual results will be the final judge, including assurance that all assumptions are in keeping with real world implementation.

(3)Maintaining consistent methodologies

Across an organization, for various decisions and products and services, it is important that a forecasting consistency be maintained. This is an important part of managing the forecasting process. If various decisions are made on a piecemeal basis with no consistency, then organizational priorities will not be properly established and resources will be allocated improperly.

(4) Tracking actuals against the forecasts

The ultimate test of a forecast is when actual results come in and can be compared to the forecast. But of course the assumptions made and documented in the buy-in process must also have been achieved. For example, if at the last minute, someone reduces the promotion and advertising or training or servicing for an offering, then it will be difficult to achieve the sales that were forecast unless some other assumption is exceeded.

(5) Publicize the forecast requirements of the organizational entity

Lastly, the forecasting staff must let the entire organization know the importance of a valid forecast in making any decisions. This can be done by publicizing the overall forecasting process and the requirements for a valid forecast. But individual forecast numbers and details must always be held in strict confidence and the entire organization must be aware of security in regard to forecasts. It is completely acceptable for an organization's forecast organization to "toot their horn" in this regard. The worst case is when the forecast process remains secret and mysterious, which will inhibit the required cross-organizational support.

*****

EPILOGUE

Individuals and organizations never fully reveal what they will do in the future. They can't. They *"don't know everything about the future environment,"* and don't want to commit to a course of action. They might change their minds. *"Other things might come up."*

But this should not stop us from asking an individual or an organization what they think *at this point in time* about something. Then we can include the response in our plans for the future. This is called forecasting from market research.

This short book should help those courageous enough to put together forecasts that support decisions. Just remember that your work is not perfect and that we do the best that we can do to team with others in these endeavors.

*****

APPENDIX A

LEGACY HISTORICAL STATISTICAL ANALYSIS & TRENDING

"...hindsight as foresight makes no sense."
W.H. Auden, poet, 1907-1973

"Far better an approximate answer to the right question, which is often vague, than an exact answer to the wrong question, which can always be made precise."
John Tukey, mathematician, 1915-2000

A.1 - STATISTICAL FORECASTING IN PERSPECTIVE

The first thing many analysts want to do is to "get some data" and then start manipulating the data in their favorite software. If you don't think this is true, then go to any online search engine and put in the word "forecasting" and you will get thousands of items having to do with plugging data into software. In fact, to some, the term forecasting automatically means statistical analysis and trending of some

previous historical data. But where did the data come from? It is a record of *past events*, and in fact many statistical routines don't work well unless you have over 60 data points, which in annual time series is going back five years. Of course, it could be only five months and someone wants to project ahead only one or two months, and look for any deviations or cycles in this short term data. That's short term trending and should be distinguished from actual forecasting per se. In any case, how do they know that a lot of conditions haven't changed even over several months, that is, things that are not in the past data?

Many will divide *"forecasting"* into two main categories: *Quantitative Forecasting* and *Qualitative Forecasting*. Under Quantitative forecasting they will include all of the historical statistical methods (as will be described in this Appendix), and under Qualitative forecasting they will list merely judgmental methods. Totally excluded is forecasting based on market and operational models, including secondary and primary market research, and data mining of the latest environmental, demographic, and economic information.

Statistical analysis is closely related to the two areas called *"system identification"* and *"black box analysis"* in that any additional knowledge about the actual process or historical nature of the data is either unknown or ignored. For example, someone doing a statistical analysis type of forecast for some retail food chain data will ignore the

155

obvious effects that are embedded in the data set for variables like: Seasonal food buying habits, promotion and advertising, special offers and couponing, price increases or decreases, branding changes, merchandising (shelf facings, displays, store layout), store locations, fads, cultural tastes, demographics, and so forth. The data are accepted as-is and the task is to basically see how the data fit a line or a curve or some other mathemetical function, and to find the errors in fitting such a function. Then once this function is determined, the "great-leap assumption" is made that the future will look like the past and will follow this function.

As emphasized earlier in this book, the most important forecasts are for when things change, and the past data by itself can lead to incorrect forecasts and decisions. And of course, as in the case of an entirely new innovation, *there is no data*, so there is nothing to plug into the software. In such cases, frustrated analysts might improperly try to use data from other "analog" products or services from the past, but again this approach will usually lead to incorrect forecasts and wrong decisions.

There is no substitute for understanding the market and the operational environment and fully incorporating this knowledge into any forecast. Statistical analysis of the past, if relevant, can at times provide a guide to the *forecast base*, that is, the starting point for identifying target segments, but again demographics and market activity and economics of the past usually do not provide a very

156

good forecast base for the future.

Over many years, methods to try to predict the future from historical data have been developed. This has almost been like the middle ages "alchemy" effort to turn lead into gold. In fact, it has been said that more was published about alchemy than any other subject, and equally over the years, publications on historical forecasting have been voluminous. One of the earliest "forecasting" works was the "Divination" writings of the Roman Emporer Cicero in 45 B.C. Incredibly, there was and still is an interest in horoscopes and astrology to try to predict the future.

The truth is that historical statistical trending merely can reveal patterns in the data, like cycles, or correlations between different data sets, and that with the assumption that the "*past will repeat itself*" then a forecast can be produced. This assumption is often used when the forecaster knows nothing about the market or operations, or does not want to try to find out because of organizational separation, lack or knowledge, or lack of skill. For example, in some organizations, financial groups produce projections using only past financial data and statistical methods, without regard to marketing, operations, or the environment. This is a dangerous and unnecessary approach.

Let us say that someone wants to know the human resources requirements, namely retail clerks and support staff, that will be needed in the upcoming Christmas season. They know from past data that during the Christmas season from Labor Day until New Years, sales have increased on the average of 20% per week over the average week of the year, so they assume that retail clerk requirements should increase equally. They make this 20% recommendation to human resources hiring managers. However, they are unaware that this retail chain has redesigned their website, and also instituted a major partnership with Amazon, and also contracted with Google for an increase in online ads for the Christmas season. And also those making the 20% hiring recommendation do not know that product managers in this retail chain have done a profitabiity analysis and found that they have a better margin with online sales than they do for in-store sales, because of a number of overhead and supply chain factors. The retail chain goes ahead and hires more clerks for Christmas, but ends up paying for a lot of extra people who just stand around talking to each other. They don't find about the error until much later in the next year when they analyze their channel mix and Christmas sales. They just blame the error on "increased online sales" because customers like the Internet. The retail chain could have avoided the hiring error by developing a simple forecast model that included the channel mix assumptions, plus awareness and promotion targeting, and coordinating all of this through a team effort. Even better, a team effort could have been in charge of Christmas programs and a Christmas business case, and recommended incentives to drive customers to the optimal channel mix, in the face of competition, taking into account and modeling a number of different Christmas scenarios.

The bottom line here is that usually the most important forecasts are when things change, either because of the direct actions of a company or institution or individual, or because of changes in the environment, including things that might have changed because of competitive actions or regulatory or legislative actions.

The Failure of Purely Linear Trending

We often think of simple linear regression as a tool for trending that will behave as follows in the plot below.

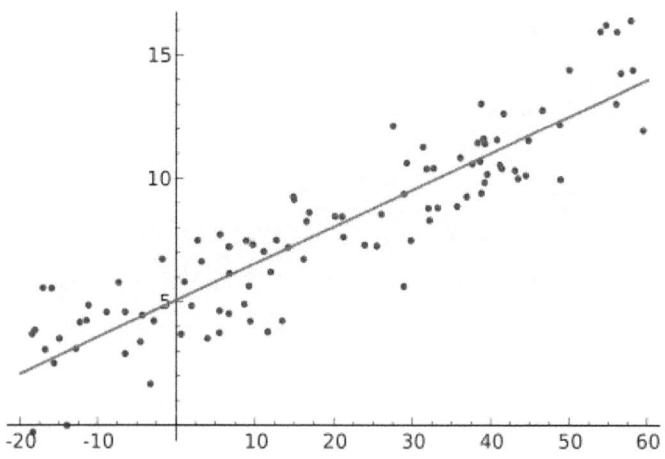

(https://en.wikipedia.org/wiki/Linear_regression#Least-squares_estimation_and_related_techniques)

Most often the line through the data is fitted to minimize the sum of the squares of the differences in the dependent variable, between the line and the data points, and this is called OLS (*Ordinary Least Squares*).

But although pure linear trending of data might seem like the first thing to do when presented with a set of historical information, this can lead to some incorrect, and even hilarious conclusions. The statistician Francis "Frank" Anscombe (1918-2001) demonstrated this fact via what is known as the "Anscombe's Quartet" which is the following four entirely different graphed data sets, but which all have the exact same linear regression result. (*Reference 8*).

Anscombe's quartet

I		II		III		IV	
x	y	x	y	x	y	x	y
10.0	8.04	10.0	9.14	10.0	7.46	8.0	6.58
8.0	6.95	8.0	8.14	8.0	6.77	8.0	5.76
13.0	7.58	13.0	8.74	13.0	12.74	8.0	7.71
9.0	8.81	9.0	8.77	9.0	7.11	8.0	8.84
11.0	8.33	11.0	9.26	11.0	7.81	8.0	8.47
14.0	9.96	14.0	8.10	14.0	8.84	8.0	7.04
6.0	7.24	6.0	6.13	6.0	6.08	8.0	5.25
4.0	4.26	4.0	3.10	4.0	5.39	19.0	12.50
12.0	10.84	12.0	9.13	12.0	8.15	8.0	5.56
7.0	4.82	7.0	7.26	7.0	6.42	8.0	7.91
5.0	5.68	5.0	4.74	5.0	5.73	8.0	6.89

When the simple linear regression results ot these four data sets in the above table are graphed, they look like this:

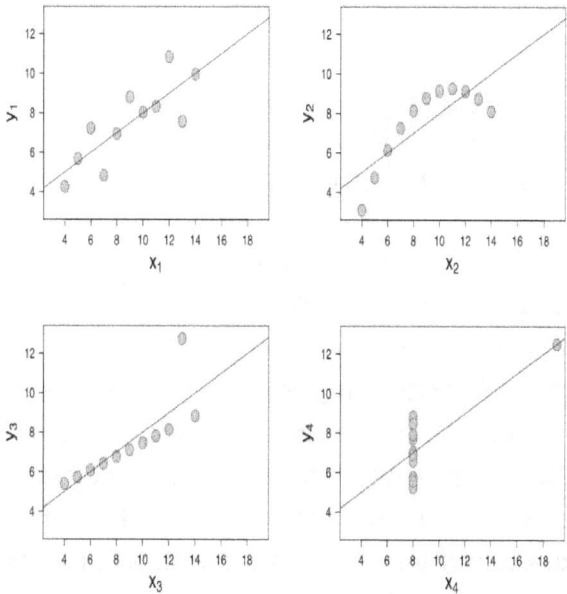

The point here is that simply applying an algorithm to some data without first taking a look at the data, especially graphically, is not useful in trying to trend the data correctly.

A.2 STATISTICAL FORECASTING METHODOLOGIES

There are many ways to categorize the methodologies used for historical statistical analysis and forecasting, but first it is useful to state some of the terminology that is used in these methodologies. Please note that this Section is merely a review because this is not the principal subject of this book.

Stationarity is assumed or required in many statistical analysis algorithms, and it is defined as a set of data for one variable over a time period, that is called a time-series, for which the *mean* (simple unweighted average) and the *variance* (the average of the squared differences from the mean), and the *autocorrelation* (the repetitive nature in the pattern of the data over time, for a particular time lag) are all constant throughout the time series period. The probability distribution of a stationary process remains constant over time. Stationarity basically means that the pattern of the data remains the same over time, and that some underlying process which has produced that data has remained constant over that prior time period. For the purpose of forecasting historical data, if stationarity is assumed, then the future will follow the same pattern as the past, and this makes the forecasting quite simple.

Non-Stationarity means that the time series data do not meet the above definition of stationarity, basically meaning that the pattern of the data does not repeat itself over time, and therefore the underlying process which produced the data is changing with time. Most processes in nature and the environment are non-stationary and have a random distribution of some sort. Many of the man-made processes attempt to be essentially stationary and repetitive, with hopefully only small deviations from true stationarity. There are many ways to try to convert a non-stationary time series to a stationary one, such as *differencing* (creating a new time series which is merely the difference between successive data points, and this can be done one or more times). Another possible way to transform a non-stationary time series to a stationary time series is to apply a transformation function, such as a logarithmic transformation. And one can find a linear trend in the data and subtract this trend out of the data and sometimes the residual leftovers will then be stationary. Obviously, after the statistical analysis is performed on any resulting stationary data, then the reverse of the transformation or differencing needs to be applied to get back to a set of data that then can be used for a forecast of the future.

Time series means a single-variable collection of data, measured at even time intervals. For example, the sales of a product at the end of every month for the last five years, or the population of the U.S. at the end of the year for the last ten years.

ARIMA is the acronym for an Autoregressive Integrated Moving Average type of statistical analysis model.

Often the following statistical categories to model historical data are stated:

Smoothing Models: These are simple models like *moving average* (the average of past data as it changes).

Curve Fitting Models: Again a simple idea, curve fitting merely is finding a mathematical function that will fit past data, within a certain error accuracy, and then using this model to predict future values. And again, forecast errors could be large.

Univariate Box-Jenkins ARIMA Models: (George Box and Gwilym Jenkins, Reference 7) These are time-series models for fitting prior data, denoted by the functions ARIMA(p,d,q), where p=the order of the autoregressive model, d=the degree of differencing, and q=the order of the moving average model. The Box-Jenkins models assume that the data are stationary, after any differencing or transformation.

Box-Jenkins Intervention Models: These are modification of the above Box-Jenkins time-series models by adding in an additional function, such as a pulse or a step function or something else, to try to account for something in the historical data which has caused a significant deviation. In the historical data, at a particular known time, the *mean* of the data will have changed due to some event, and so this change is then incorporated in the model. However, the assumption is made that the ARIMA model both before and after this change in the *mean* will be the same. The approximate time of the change in the mean can be identified by graphing the data, and the mean could change in several ways, either a shift to a new permanent mean, or a temporary shift in the mean and then return to the original mean, and this change could be sudden or gradual and either an increase or decrease in the mean value.

Transfer Function Models: The term transfer function comes from signal processing in engineering, such as the input-output relationship of a circuit in electrical engineering, using the Laplace transform. TFN (transfer function noise) models can be used for statistical analysis of historical data, and then when the transfer function is identified, it can be used to create a forecast.

Frequency Response Models: Also from engineering signal analysis or *system identification*, these types of models utilize the Fourier Transform to identify the cosine function series for both the input and the output. Theoretically, a Fourier analysis can model virtually any type of data if the Fourier series is extended sufficiently, and then a forecast can be generated with the usual assumption that the past predicts the future.

Kalman Filter: is a linear signal filtering and prediction algorithm (named after the electrical engineer and professor Rudolph Kalman, b.5-19-30) which is used to extract a signal from an incomplete collection of noisy data. The algorithm makes a number of assumptions, including Bayesian inference to "fill in the data." Kalman filtering has been used in many engineering and space program applications, and can be used in trying to identify historical information.

A.3 STATISTICAL TRENDING AND THE FORECAST BASE

There are times when trending and purely statistical forecasting does have an important place in several regards. First. although they are not market or strategic forecasting, demographic census statistics and

165

projections, regarding current age segments and cultural and racial segment shifts, are often very useful in projecting the *forecast base* that will exist in the future. Of course, birth rates, household composition, and a number of other assumptions go into these census projections. With the very robust assumption that those in a certain age group today will live throughout a normal life cycle, barring any catastrophic health or cultural or social change, this projection of age groups can help us understand future behavior. Of course, we have to make a number of assumptions about how different age groups and cultural and ethnic and racial groups behave today and will behave in the future.

The U.S. Department of Commerce, which oversees the U.S. Census and the BEA (Bureau of Economic Analysis), has many time series that can aid in establishing the proper forecast base for forecast model development. (Note: See Appendix B for this and other fundamental data sources.) This is where you can start with the most basic forecast base information, like how many households are in the U.S., or how many cars are sold each year, or what are the expenditures for clothing, either at the national or state or county level, all the way down to a ZIP code. But before using any of this data, you must have established *target market segments*. For example, you are not going to start a forecast for an over-the-counter non-prescription drug with the entire population of the U.S. as the base for the forecast.

*****

APPENDIX B

SOME SECONDARY RESEARCH AND DATA MINING SOURCES

1. **Statistical Abstract of the U.S.**
   https://catalog.data.gov/dataset/statistical-abstract-of-the-united-states **and**
   http://www.census.gov/library/publications/time-series/statistical_abstracts.html
   "First published in 1878, the Statistical Abstract serves as the official federal summary of statistics and provides over 1,400 tables of benchmark measures on the demographic, housing, social, political, and economic condition of the United States." "The U.S. Census Bureau terminated the collection of data for the Statistical Compendia program effective October 1, 2011. The Statistical Compendia program is comprised of the Statistical Abstract of the United States and its supplemental products—the State and Metropolitan Area Data Book and the County and City Data Book."

2. **U.S. Dept. of Commerce - BEA (Bureau of Economic Analysis)** http://www.bea.gov/
   "The Bureau of Economic Analysis (BEA) produces economic accounts statistics that enable

government and business decision makers, researchers, and the American public to follow and understand the performance of the Nation's economy." The BEA NIPA (National Income and Product Accounts) Tables show quarterly U.S. data for the last three years, for things like personal income, and personal goods & services expenditures. They also keep track of U.S. GDP by industry segment.

3. **U.S. Dept. of Commerce - Census Bureau**
   http://www.census.gov/
   "The Census Bureau is part of the U.S. Dept. of Commerce. The U.S. Census Bureau is overseen by the Economics and Statistics Administration (ESA) within the Department of Commerce. The Economics and Statistics Administration provides high-quality economic analysis and fosters the missions of the U.S. Census Bureau and the BEA." As an example the Census "Quick Facts" shows a number of U.S. population, household, housing, age, and income segments, many down to the ZIP code level.

4. **U.S. Dept. of Commerce - ESA (Economics and Statistics Administration)**
   http://www.esa.gov/
   "The Economics and Statistics Administration (ESA) provides timely economic analysis, disseminates national economic indicators, and serves as the administrator of the Department's premiere statistical programs. ESA manages the U.S. Census Bureau (Census), the Bureau of

168

Economic Analysis (BEA), and the Office of the Chief Economist (OCE). Census collects, BEA compiles and OCE analyzes the most comprehensive, consistent, confidential, credible and publicly available socio economic data on our nation's economy, businesses and individuals."

5. U.S Bureau of Labor Statistics, in the U.S. Dept. of Labor http://www.bls.gov/bls/infohome.htm
"The Bureau of Labor Statistics of the U.S. Department of Labor is the principal Federal agency responsible for measuring labor market activity, working conditions, and price changes in the economy. Its mission is to collect, analyze, and disseminate essential economic information to support public and private decision-making. As an independent statistical agency, BLS serves its diverse user communities by providing products and services that are objective, timely, accurate, and relevant."

5. U.S. DEPT OF LABOR, BUREAU OF LABOR STATISTICS (BLS)
AMERICAN TIME USE SURVEY (ATUS)
http://www.bls.gov/tus/home.html
"The American Time Use Survey (ATUS) measures the amount of time people spend doing various activities, such as paid work, childcare, volunteering, and socializing."

6. U.S. DEPT OF LABOR, BUREAU OF LABOR STATISTICS (BLS)
CONSUMER EXPENDITURES SURVEY

http://www.bls.gov/cex/

"The Consumer Expenditure Survey (CE) program consists of two surveys, the Quarterly Interview Survey and the Diary Survey, that provide information on the buying habits of American consumers, including data on their expenditures, income, and consumer unit (families and single consumers) characteristics. The survey data are collected for the Bureau of Labor Statistics by the U.S. Census Bureau." "The CE is important because it is the only Federal survey to provide information on the complete range of consumers' expenditures and incomes, as well as the characteristics of those consumers. It is used by economic policymakers examining the impact of policy changes on economic groups, by the Census Bureau as the source of thresholds for the Supplemental Poverty Measure, by businesses and academic researchers studying consumers' spending habits and trends, by other Federal agencies, and, perhaps most importantly, to regularly revise the Consumer Price Index market basket of goods and services and their relative importance."

7. **Gartner** *"Gartner, Inc. (NYSE: IT) is the world's leading information technology research and advisory company. We deliver the technology-related insight necessary for our clients to make the right decisions, every day."*
   http://www.gartner.com/technology/about.jsp

8. **Forrester** *"Forrester (Nasdaq: FORR) is one of the most influential research and advisory firms in the world. We work with business and technology leaders to develop customer-obsessed strategies that drive growth. Forrester's unique insights are grounded in annual surveys of more than 500,000 consumers and business leaders worldwide, rigorous and objective methodologies, and the shared wisdom of our most innovative clients. Through proprietary research, data, custom consulting, exclusive executive peer groups, and events, the Forrester experience is about a singular and powerful purpose: to challenge the thinking of our clients to help them lead change in their organizations." https://www.forrester.com/home/* **Forrester publishes thousands of secondary research reports on virtually every industry segment, and also does client custom market research and consulting.**

7. Teradata *http://www.teradata.com/*

"You've got data. Lots of data. Human-, machine-, business- and interaction-generated data. And more of it becomes available every second of every day. But if you can't find the customer and business insights within your data, it just remains untapped potential. That's where we can help. At Teradata, we provide end-to-end solutions and services in data warehousing, big data and analytics, and marketing applications that enable you to become a data-driven business...one that's positioned to increase revenue, improve

efficiency, and create the most compelling experience for your customers. After all, your business is about your customers. So is ours."

7. Statista http://www.statista.com/aboutus/

"Statista is one of the leading statistics companies on the internet. With a team of over 250 statisticians, database experts, analysts, and editors, Statista provides users with an innovative and intuitive tool for researching quantitative data, statistics and related information. The product is aimed at business clients and academics of any size. Consultant firms and media agencies license our services as well as strategy and marketing departments in large corporations from a variety of industries. Our client base includes a wide range of globally active companies and premier academic institutions. Since the launch of the platform in 2008, more than 750,000 users have registered with Statista."

7. Report Linker http://www.reportlinker.com/

"ReportLinker is a technology company that simplifies how analysts and decision makers get industry data for their business thanks to: latest reports & slideshows with insights from top research analysts that provide full understanding of how 5,000+ industry sectors work (industry overview, key players, market drivers...) 24 Million easily actionable statistics with tables, figures & datasets (sales forecasts, market shares, production data...) More than 10,000 trusted

sources such as government agencies, international organizations, consultancies, industry associations..."

7. Oracle and Datalogix http://www.oracle.com/
Oracle acquired Datalogix and added them to their DataCloud service. *"Datalogix connects offline purchasing data to digital media to improve audience targeting and measure sales impact. Datalogix aggregates and provides insights on over $2 trillion in consumer spending to deliver purchase-based targeting and drive more sales. Over 650 customers including the top US advertisers and digital media publishers use Datalogix to increase the effectiveness and measurability of their advertising."*

9. Encyclopedia of American Industries
http://www.referenceforbusiness.com/#ixzz43mVF7 qv2
"Our Encyclopedia of Small Business is a comprehensive and easily accessible reference source for entrepreneurs that demand practical information that can be applied to their own business. Small business owners can browse over the 600 articles that detail information about financial planning, market analysis, sales, business plans, tax planning, human resource issues and more." "Our Business Biographies are a superb tool for biographical information of industry leaders worldwide. We have over 600 in-depth essays that cover each individual's biographical

information, career paths, achievements, leadership strategies and management styles." "The Business Plans section is composed of actual business plans written by entrepreneurs in North America who are seeking financing for their business. This is a great resource for anybody needing examples on how to structure, compose, and write their own business plans." "Finally, the Encyclopedia of American Industries is a comprehensive guide to industries in every realm of American business. We cover 459 manufacturing industries, and have over 500 essays about non-manufacturing and service industries."

10. **ENTREPRENEURSHIP.ORG**

http://www.entrepreneurship.org/resource-center/secondary-market-research-resources.aspx

"Before you launch or expand your business venture, you need to understand your industry, your competitors, and your customers. While specific data is often gathered by conducting primary research through tools such as interviews and focus groups, performing secondary market research can be as easy as heading to the business section of your local library." "You'll find a wealth of information collected and published by organizations such as trade associations, government agencies, and commercial publishers. Detailed below are some fundamental secondary research resources, which are either online or library-accessible, to help you analyze your market."

11. EBSCO *https://www.ebscohost.com/*

"Because EBSCO Information Services is a part of the information technology community, our needs are those of our customers. We're dedicated to developing customizable services, supporting the technology needs of our customers and creating strong user experiences to help libraries and other institutions support their end users and improve access to information." "EBSCOhost databases are the most-used, premium online information resources for tens of thousands of institutions worldwide, representing millions of end users."

12. PROQUEST *http://www.proquest.com/*

"ProQuest is committed to empowering researchers and librarians around the world. Its innovative information content and technologies increase the productivity of students, scholars, professionals and the libraries that serve them. Through partnerships with content holders, ProQuest preserves rich, vast and varied information – whether historical archives or today's scientific breakthroughs – and packages it with digital technologies that enhance its discovery, sharing and management. For academic, corporate, government, school and public libraries, as well as professional researchers, ProQuest provides services that enable strategic acquisition, management and discovery of information collections."

175

13. **DUN&BRADSTREET** *http://www.dnb.com/*

"Our platform's foundation is the world's largest commercial database, with over 240 million company records we derive from 30,000 data sources, trade data from more than 1 billion accounts receivable records and update 5 million times per day. We integrate this insight into your core systems, workflows and cloud-based apps in ways that enhance their impact, and we also integrate with your existing data and third-party data sources. Our DUNSRight® process gives us the unmatched ability to turn an enormous stream of data into the high-quality information you need to grow your most valuable relationships.".

14. **DUN&BRADSTREET ZAPPDATA (mailing lists)**
https://www.dnb.com/product/tour/zapdata.htm
"zapdata allows you to find the U.S. companies you want by specifying the criteria the businesses must meet. Select links(s) in the top frame or body of the page to search by Locations, Industries, Demographics, Specialty Data, or Job Function. Enter your search criteria. Preview your selections."

15. *REFERENCEUSA http://www.referenceusa.com/*
"ReferenceUSA is the leading provider in business and consumer research! Offering a full-service platform, ReferenceUSA helps users create marketing plans, conduct competitive analysis, raise funds and locate people. Our database

selections and real-time access to more than 24 Million Businesses, 262 Million Consumers, U.S. New Businesses, U.S. New Homeowners and Movers, make research easy and fast! ReferenceUSA's quality information helps researchers, students and job-seekers answer a wide variety of questions, and saves them valuable time and money."

16. A.C. NIELSEN: NIELSEN SEGMENTATION AND MARKET SOLUTIONS

https://segmentationsolutions.nielsen.com/consum eractivation/Default.jsp?ID=self-register

"In a fast moving, content rich marketplace, it is often difficult to get the attention of your core customers. Nielsen Segmentation & Market Solutions is an extremely robust and easy to use tool that incorporates everything you need into one convenient platform. Gain immediate access to the Quick Market Insights and Quick Market Insights Advanced packages, and associated add-on data, by following the steps below."

17. MANTA *http://www.manta.com/*

"Manta is one of the largest online resources dedicated to small business. We deliver products, services and educational opportunities that are effective, easy to understand and geared to help business owners become more competitive in their respective industries." "The Manta directory boasts millions of unique visitors every month who search our comprehensive database for individual

businesses, industry segments and geographic-specific listings. Business owners can claim and customize their page to improve online visibility and marketability, gain key knowledge vital for success, and find products to help grow and manage their business. The Manta team works hard to deliver effective <u>educational resources, promotion opportunities and tools</u> for small businesses"

18. *http://www.digitalbusinessmodelguru.com/* **This website, while not authoritative, discusses business models for a number of companies and industries.**

*****

APPENDIX C

SOME SOFTWARE FOR MARKET RESEARCH, FORECASTING, AND BUSINESS CASES

The following lists of software packages, platforms, and cloud services are offered without endorsement, but most of these have been reviewed positively by others and by actual users. Descriptions in quotations are from the web links listed, and the listing order is purely random. In many cases there are free downloads and free evaluation copies, and many of these have both panel and individual respondent features available. It is recommended that readers interested in any of these obtain an evaluation copy and determine if the software is suitable for the particular project that they are undertaking.

APPENDIX C.1 SOME MARKET RESEARCH SOFTWARE

(1) Voxco's Multimode Survey Software
http://www.voxco.com/
"Powerful survey software for a multi-channel world. Maximize your organization's survey efficiency. Run any type of survey across multiple channels into one

centralized platform."

(2) NEBU's DUB Interviewer Software
http://www.nebu.com/

"Our purpose is to help our clients and users to continuously increase the efficiency of their Market Research processes with our innovative products and outstanding support." " ... Our products are constantly developed under our scrum process, so we can deliver new features, or react to market changes, quickly and easily. ..."

(3) Key Survey by WorldAPP https://www.keysurvey.com/
"Survey Software For Mid to Large Organizations; Mobile, Online and Offline Data Collection For Every Survey Process"

(4) Key Survey by WorldAPP https://www.keysurvey.com/
"Survey Software For Mid to Large Organizations; Mobile, Online and Offline Data Collection For Every Survey Process"

(5) Checkbox Survey   https://www.checkbox.com/
"Professional Survey Software at an Affordable Pric. Whether you're a two-person startup or a Fortune 500, Checkbox delivers powerful, secure online surveys and data collection tools. Hosted or Installable."

(6) BRAND24 Market Research Software
https://brand24.com/

[This is an online and mobile monitoring app]
"30,000 Monitored brands all over the world: A powerful award-winning app for social media monitoring; start free trial"

(7) Question PRO Survey Software
http://www.questionpro.com/

"Quickly create online surveys and polls with our intuitive web based software tool. You can create your own survey, copy a professionally written survey template, or upload your survey directly from a Word file. "

(8) Creative Research System Survey System
http://www.surveysystem.com/

"Survey Software - The Survey System; Software for Web Surveys, Mobile Surveys, Telephone Interviews; The Survey System is the most complete survey software package available for all types of questionnaires and research projects from web, telephone, mobile, CAPI, or paper questionnaires. This exceptional survey software package is ideal for mixrd-mode surveys, which combine two or more of those methods."

(9) Tellwut Market Research
https://www.tellwut.com/online-survey-solutions

"Online Surveys have become a reliable feedback platform enabling businesses to crowdsource insights from their stakeholders and are an extremely effective method to achieve better results. At Tellwut you can also utilize our panel to conduct online market research. Try our Free Trial today or contact us for a DIY Online Market Research Web Survey Quote!"

(10) Qualtrics Research Suite

https://www.qualtrics.com/research-suite/

"Fast insights for markets that won't stand still; When you want your products to be as innovative as the artists who use them, you need an insight platform that's fast and flexible enough to put the customer's voice into every step of the development."

(11) Research Reporter by FocusVision

https://www.focusvision.com/products/researchreporter/

"ResearchReporter is a powerful, integrated research management platform that provides deeper insights to turn your research into a competitive advantage. View previous research, automate and streamline processes, and manage resources — including vendors and budgets — all in one place."

(12) Amplitude Research Solutions

http://www.amplituderesearch.com/

"10+ years serving clients throughout the United States! Amplitude Research® provides high-quality mail, telephone, and online survey research for consumer and b2b market research surveys, employee job satisfaction surveys, and all types of customer satisfaction, loyalty and feedback surveys. Our research services include questionnaire writing, survey hosting, survey administration, data analysis, and report writing."

(13) ARCS by Marketing Systems Group

http://www.m-s-g.com/Web/arcs/market-research.aspx

"There are a number of reasons why having the

ARCS® IVR and Web modules as options in your market research endeavors can be beneficial: Collect data without incurring the incremental costs of interviewers; Collect sensitive data (many respondents are reluctant to divulge sensitive data to interviewers – the IVR or Web system can put them at ease)."

(14) Comfirmit
https://www.confirmit.com/

"Our Mission; We leverage our considerable, proven and scalable multimode data collection and reporting capabilities to provide our corporate and Market Research customers with a more holistic view of their customers' and employees' experience and journey within their organization."

(15) Custom Panels & Portals by FGI Research
http://www.fgiresearch.com/

"Our Mission; At FGI Research & Analytics, our mission is to help you make faster and better decisions so you can achieve greater success in an increasingly competitive world. We've helped hundreds of leading companies achieve better results. ...":

(16) DataPlay by Margasoft
http://www.margasoft.com/Products/DP_Web_Portal

"DataPlay Web Portal is an integrated all-in-1 tool, which fully meets your analysis, visualization and presentation needs. It is simple, intuitive and can significantly cut your time spent on analysis and presentation of data."

(17) EFS Panel by QuestBack

https://www.questback.com/data-hub-panels

"The Questback Data Hub and Panel module is the workhorse of our enterprise feedback platform. Its scalable database combines powerful panel administration and a content management system for designing portal websites and communities.

(18) FlexMR Research Platform

https://www.flexmr.net/

"World leading online market research; Built by research experts, Flex^{MR} is the world's most advanced online research platform. Now, it can be yours too."

(19) Handrail

http://www.handrailux.com/

"Define, Measure & Improve User Experience; Handrail is a collaborative interviewing tool for customer discovery, concept testing and usability assessments."

(20) Opinion-Central from InsightExpress

https://www.opinion-central.com/AboutUs.aspx

"Opinion-Central is InsightExpress' actively-managed proprietary panel. On this site members can: View and modify panelist information, Take a survey, See selected survey results, Read interesting facts, Participate in polls – coming soon!"

(21) Instantly (now Survey Sampling International, LLC.)

https://www.surveysampling.com/

"SSI is the premier global provider of data solutions and technology to drive business success. Over

2,500 companies worldwide trust SSI to power the insights that grow their business. We offer consumer and B2B survey research, reaching respondents in 100+ countries via Internet, telephone, mobile/wireless and mixed-access offerings. ..."

(22) Kinesis Panel by Kinesis Survey Technologies
http://www.kinesissurvey.com/

"Market Research Tools for Tomorrow; Tackle your market research projects like a pro; KinesisPanel market research software and solutions combine powerful quantitative and qualitative tools with a high-performance cloud based platform. ..."

APPENDIX C.2 SOME FORECASTING SOFTWARE

(1) Demand Foresight's Demand Commander Software
http://www.demandforesight.com/forecasting-and-planning-software/

"Our Forecasting and Planning software suite supports the complete Sales and Operations Planning process, but with one key difference: It is driven by the most accurate forecasting engine in the marketplace; Download 6-page solution overview. ..."

(2) Vanguard Software
http://www.vanguardsw.com/business-forecasting-101/forecasting-methods-models-techniques/

"Vanguard Software delivers the sharpest forecasting and optimization software in the world –

benchmark verified. Small wonder considering we're one of the only leaders in advanced analytics to focus on predictive technologies. We don't just reveal the future, we help you shape it."

(3) NCSS

http://www.ncss.com/software/ncss/time-series-and-forecasting-in-ncss/

"NCSS contains an array of tools for time series and forecasting, including ARIMA, spectral analysis, decomposition forecasting, and exponential smoothing. Each time series and forecasting procedure is straightforward to use and validated for accuracy. Use the links below to jump to a specific time series / forecasting topic. For more details about a particular procedure, we recommend you download and install the free trial of the software."

(4) QUANTRIX

https://www.quantrix.com/en/sample-models/data-modeling-techniques/

"Quantrix Modeler; By addressing the limitations and risks inherent to spreadsheets when developing business-critical models, Quantrix allows you to tap into the collective expertise of your team. It offers unmatched capability for forecasting, planning, budgeting, risk modeling and visual analytics, and also allows you to develop 'what if' scenarios and model the financial and operational impact of business decisions."

(5) SAS

http://www.sas.com/en_ph/software/analytics/forecastserver.html

SAS® Forecast Server; Forecasting software that automatically generates large numbers of high-quality forecasts"

(6) Forecast PRO

http://www.forecastpro.com/products/overview/method.htm

"With ForecastPro, you can create accurate forecasts quickly and easily using proven statistical forecasting methods. ..."

(7) Adaptive Insights

http://www.adaptiveinsights.com/products/adaptive-planning

"Unshackle your budgeting, planning, and forecasting from risky spreadsheet-centric processes with cloud-based planning software proven to accelerate productivity by more than 70%. Integrate revenue and expense planning, power rolling forecasts, and analyze performance."

(8) Tagetik

http://www.tagetik.com/us/software/modeling-forecasting

"Changing economic, environment, market and industry events continue to create risk and ongoing volatility. That's why Tagetik provides business modeling, 'what-if' scenario playing and forecasting within its unified corporate performance management solution." "Using Tagetik modeling and forecasting software, users can

easily assess different business scenarios and instantly see the impact on financial performance and generate rolling forecasts with the click of a button."

(9) LookAhead from Argus Predictive Analytics

http://www.strategicanalytics.com/prod_lookahead.php

"LookAhead is configurable to enhance business function across the organization: Loss and Delinquency Forecasting, Portfolio Stress Testing, Collections & Recovery Forecasting, Marketing and Originations Performance, Profitability Forecasting"

(10) Prophix

http://www.prphix.coProphixm/capabilities/business-modeling/

"Create models for all types of business requirements in one product. Whether you work for a small organization or a large multinational, your company needs to develop business models that track your performance at varying levels of detail. Using spreadsheets or developing customized models with data from multiple sources requires specialized skills and sophisticated knowledge of IT systems. Documenting the logic and data flow in these custom models is next to impossible...."

(11) InsightSquared

http://www.insightsquared.com/features/sales-forecasting/

"The Holistic Company Forecast; Contrast Forecast Results; There are many methods you can use to forecast. Contrasting multiple models is a proven way to arrive at a reliable forecast. ..."

(12) JustEnough

http://www.justenough.com/demand-forecasting-software/

    "Demand Forecasting Software" ... "An end-to-end process, demand forecasting is not a stand-alone activity. The fact is that actual customer demand needs to drive the entire business, as consumers today are more sophisticated, fickle and have many more options than just traditional brick & mortar – which used to be the only choice available. ..."

APPENDIX C.3 SOME BUSINESS CASE SOFTWARE

(1) Business Survival Toolkit

http://business-survival-toolkit.co.uk/stage-three/business-case-development/developing-a-robust-business-case

    "A business case is a means of providing evidence that a project is a good investment for your business and/or an external investor. It differs from a business plan in that it focuses on a specific project or programme rather than the whole business. It is effectively an investment tool that sells a particular idea or concept. Downloadable PDF Tool ..."

(2) Solution Matrix Limited

https://www.business-case-analysis.com/business-case.html

    "Business case analysis BCA can be defined as a decision support and planning tool that projects the likely financial results and other business consequences of an action. The analysis essentially asks "What happens if we take this or that action?" The analysis answers in

business terms—business costs, <u>business benefits</u>, and business risks. ..."

(3) Software Engineering Institute, Carnegie Mellon University

http://www.sei.cmu.edu/productlines/consulting/businessc ase/

"Business Case Development; A business case answers key questions. Organizations must develop a business case to address those questions when planning the transition to the product line approach to fielding software systems. ..."

(4) University of Cambridge

http://www.inclusivedesigntoolkit.com/betterdesign2/busin esscase/businesscase.html

"Business case materials; It is often necessary to produce a business case for inclusive design, showing the value for a business of taking on a specific inclusive design project. ..." (downloads listed)

(5) What Is - How To Write a Business Case

http://whatis.techtarget.com/reference/How-to-write-a-business-case

"A business case document is a formal, written argument intended to convince a decision maker to approve some kind of action. ..."

*****

APPENDIX D

SOME MARKET RESEARCH SUPPLIERS

Supplier Directories

(1) Market Research Association,
http://www.marketingresearch.org/
"Founded in 1957 and based in Washington, the Marketing Research Association is the leading and largest U.S. association of the opinion and marketing research profession, which delivers insights and strategies to help guide the decisions of companies providing products and services to consumers and businesses."

(2) GreenBook
http://www.greenbook.org/
"GreenBook Directory helps you find marketing research suppliers, facilities, and consultants as well as providers of related services. Browse by market research specialties or locations below to find a vendor that meets your requirements."

(3) Quirks Marketing Research Media
http://www.quirks.com/
"Directories for market research facilities, moderators, software, panels, supplier SourceBook(TM)"

(4) SurveyPolice

https://www.surveypolice.com/

"Since 2005, SurveyPolice has been a reliable and trusted source for unbiased online surveys information. With one of, if not the most comprehensive online directories of survey panels, our website is used and respected by both survey takers and market research companies alike. Best of all, our site is completely free to use!"

(5) *SurveyBounty*

http://www.surveybounty.com/

"The ultimate online survey directory"

Selected Research Suppliers

(1) Brainjuicer

http://www.brainjuicer.com/

"BrainJuicer was founded in 1999 with one goal in mind: to re-invent market research. Our Behavioural Science approach is what drives clients to seek us out when the traditional methodologies have failed them, to facilitate change within their organisations and to turn true human understanding into business advantage."

(2) TS Global

http://www.tnsglobal.com/us

"We are TNS. As one of the largest research agencies worldwide we provide insights that help you make impactful decisions that drive growth."

(3) Vision Critical
https://www.visioncritical.com/

"Sparq, our customer intelligence software, helps you engage the right customers at the right time to generate the collective wisdom you need to grow. Solve your biggest business challenges with the help of ongoing, secure customer insight through a branded insight community."

(4) Synovate was in Aegis Group and now Ipsos
http://www.ipsos.com/

"Synovate, the market research arm of Aegis Group plc, generates insights to help clients drive competitive brand, product and customer experience strategies. A truly borderless company with offices in over 60 countries, ... "

(5) Nielsen
http://www.nielsen.com/us/en.html

"Comprehensive end-to-end consumer insights for faster, smarter, better decisions to help your business grow."

(6) Anderson Analytics
http://odintext.com/
http://www.andersonconsulting.com/

"More than Market Research, Anderson Analytics is a next generation market research consultancy that leverages new technologies, such as data and text mining, with traditional market research techniques."

(7) Itracks
https://www.itracks.com/

"Innovative qualitative platforms to save you time and budget."

(8) GFK

http://www.gfk.com/

"We are GfK. We turn market and user experience research into smart business decisions."

(9) Peanut Labs

http://web.peanutlabs.com/

"We connect people. Peanut Labs connects your users with thousands of paid online surveys from leading brands and market researchers."

SECONDARY MARKET RESEARCH

(1) Gartner

http://www.gartner.com/technology/home.jsp

"Gartner offers world-class, objective insight on virtually all areas of IT. Unparalleled expertise across our wide range of solutions. A truly global (and local) perspective, with clients in more than 90 countries around the world."

(2) Hoovers

http://www.hoovers.com/

"With access to over 85 million companies worldwide and relevant, up-to-date information, Hoover's is your one-stop resource for comprehensive coverage on industries, companies and the people who lead them."

(3) Booz Allen Hamilton

http://www.boozallen.com/

"In addition to providing strategic consulting expertise, Booz Allen offers a suite of software products and tools needed to help our clients solve their most complex business challenges."

(4) McKinsey

http://www.mckinsey.com/business-functions/mckinsey-analytics/how-we-help-clients

"We bring the latest analytical techniques plus a deep understanding of industry dynamics and corporate functions to help clients create the most value from data."

*****

195

APPENDIX E

FORECASTING AND PREDICTION ERRORS
- SOME HISTORICAL EXAMPLES

1876: *"The Americans have need of the telephone, but we do not. We have plenty of messenger boys."* - William Preece, British Post Office.

1876: *"This 'telephone' has too many shortcomings to be seriously considered as a means of communication."* — William Orton, President of Western Union.

1889: *"Fooling around with alternating current (AC) is just a waste of time. Nobody will use it, ever."* — Thomas Edison

1903: *"The horse is here to stay but the automobile is only a novelty – a fad."* — President of the Michigan Savings Bank advising Henry Ford's lawyer, Horace Rackham, not to invest in the Ford Motor Company.

1929: *"Stocks have reached what looks like a permanently high plateau,"* *Irving Fisher, Professor of Economics, Yale University, October 16, 1929.*

1943: *"I think there is a world market for maybe five computers,"* *Thomas J. Watson, IBM CEO, 1943.*

196

1946: *"Television won't be able to hold on to any market it captures after the first six months. People will soon get tired of staring at a plywood box every night."* — Darryl Zanuck, 20th Century Fox.

1955: *"Nuclear powered vacuum cleaners will probably be a reality within 10 years."* — Alex Lewyt, President of the Lewyt Vacuum Cleaner Company.

1958: *"With over 50 foreign cars already on sale here, the Japanese auto industry isn't likely to carve out a big slice of the U.S. market,"* Business Week, 1958.

1959: *"Before man reaches the moon, your mail will be delivered within hours from New York to Australia by guided missiles. We stand on the threshold of rocket mail."* — Arthur Summerfield, U.S. Postmaster General.

1961: *"There is practically no chance communications space satellites will be used to provide better telephone, telegraph, television or radio service inside the United States."* — T.A.M. Craven, Federal Communications Commission (FCC) commissioner.

1966: *"Remote shopping, while entirely feasible, will flop."* — *Time Magazine, 1966.*

1977: "*There is no reason for any individual to have a computer in his home.*" [He meant a home computer for running equipment, now called IOT; but he himself had a home computer at the time.] - Ken Olsen, founder of DEC (Digital Equipment Corp.), 1977.

1981: *"640K ought to be enough for anybody,"* **Bill Gates**

1981: *"Cellular phones will absolutely not replace local wire systems."* — **Marty Cooper, inventor, 1981.**

"In 1983 and 1984, 67 new types of business personal computers were introduced to the U.S. market, and most companies were expecting explosive growth. One industry forecasting service projected an installed base of 27 million units by 1988; another predicted 28 million units by 1987. In fact, only 15 million units had been shipped by 1986. By then, many manufacturers had abandoned the PC market or gone out of business altogether. The inaccurate suppositions did not stem from a lack of forecasting techniques; regression analysis, historical trend smoothing, and others were available to all the players. Instead, they shared a mistaken fundamental assumption: that relationships driving demand in the past would continue unaltered. The companies didn't foresee changes in end-user behavior or understand their market's saturation point. None realized that history can be an unreliable guide as domestic economies become more international, new technologies emerge, and industries evolve." from the HBR article, "Four Steps to Forecast Total Market Demand," by William Barnett, HBR, July 1988 Issue.

1995: *"I predict the Internet will soon go spectacularly supernova and in 1996 catastrophically collapse."*— *Robert Metcalfe, founder of 3Com and inventor of Ethernet, writing in a 1995 InfoWorld column; he later in 1999 reportedly ground up a copy of this article in a blender and literally ate (drank) it.*

1996: *"Apple is a chaotic mess without a strategic vision and certainly no future."—TIME, February 5, 1996*

1997: *"The NeXT purchase is too little too late. Apple is already dead."*—Nathan Myhrvold, Microsoft CTO, 1997.

1997: *"I'd shut [Apple] down and give the money back to the shareholders."*—Michael Dell, founder and CEO of Dell.

2004: *"Two years from now, spam will be solved,"* World Economic Forum, 2004.

2005: *"There's just not that many videos I want to watch."* — Steve Chen, CTO and co-founder of YouTube.

2006: *"Everyone's always asking me when Apple will come out with a cell phone. My answer is, 'Probably never.'"* — David Pogue, The New York Times, 2006.

2007: *"There's no chance that the iPhone is going to get any significant market share."* — Steve Ballmer, Microsoft CEO, 2007.

*****

REFERENCES
AND
USEFUL SOURCES

1. **Marketing Research Association**
    http://www.marketingresearch.org/

    "Founded in 1957 and based in Washington, the Marketing Research Association is the leading and largest U.S. association of the opinion and marketing research profession, which delivers insights and strategies to help guide the decisions of companies providing products and services to consumers and businesses."

2. **GreenBook,** http://www.greenbook.org/
    "GreenBook Directory helps you find marketing research suppliers, facilities, and consultants as well as providers of related services. Browse by market research specialties or locations below to find a vendor that meets your requirements."

3. **American Marketing Association**
    https://www.ama.org/Pages/default.aspx
    " ... With content coming from unrivaled scholarly journals, like the Journal of Marketing, and award-winning publications, like Marketing News, the AMA offers a robust perspective that understands marketer are expected to provide both solutions for today and solutions for tomorrow. No

other organization provides more ways for marketers and academics to connect with the people and resources they need to be successful."

4. *"Five Elements to Include in a Compelling Business Case, Taking your business case from 'good to great,' "* Jan 9, 2008, Ruben Melendez, CEO & Executive Analyst, Glomark-Governan, in *Information Week.*
    http://www.industryweek.com/articles/

5. *"Good to Great: Why Some Companies Make the Leap...And Others Don't ,"* Jim Collins, Harper Business, 2001.

6. "Chapter 3, Preparing a Business Case," in *Making Smart IT Choices: Understanding Value and Risk in Government IT Investments,* © 2003 Center for Technology in Government www.ctg.albany.edu

7. "Business Case, " Wikipedia,
    https://en.wikipedia.org/wiki/Business_case

8. *"A business case captures the reasoning for initiating a project or task. It is often presented in a well-structured written document, but may also sometimes come in the form of a short verbal argument or .presentation The logic of the business case is that, whenever resources such as money or effort are consumed, they should be in support of a specific business need. ..."*

9. Anscombe, F.J. (1973), "Graphs in Statistical Analysis," American Statistician 27(1): 17-21

10. "Linear Regression" at https://en.wikipedia.org/wiki/Linear_regression#Least-squares_estimation_and_related_techniques

11. Box, George; Jenkins, Gwilym (1970). Time Series Analysis: Forecasting and Control. San Francisco: Holden-Day.

12. *"A Brief History of Decision Support Systems Version 2.1,"* by D.J.Power, DSSResources.com http://dssresources.com/history/dsshistory.html

13. *Decision Support Systems* https://en.wikipedia.org/wiki/Decision_support_system

14. *Dashboard - MIS* https://en.wikipedia.org/wiki/Executive_dashboard

*****

INDEX

*****

ABOUT THE AUTHOR

Andrew C. Merritt holds a B.S. from NYU and an M.S. from Princeton, and completed the Market Research Program at Columbia.

He was a systems engineer for the Apollo lunar landing, and has managed forecasting, market research, business development, and business plans for many situations, both domestically and internationally.

In addition to this book, *Forecasting for Market and Strategic Decisions*, he has authored *Prevail, Excel: Career Control Guide*, and the novel *Renewal: Human Excogitated.*

*****